Cambridge Elements ☰

Elements in Defence Economics
edited by
Keith Hartley
University of York

THE ECONOMICS OF CONFLICT AND PEACE

History and Applications

Shikha Basnet Silwal
Washington and Lee University

Charles H. Anderton
College of the Holy Cross

Jurgen Brauer
Chulalongkorn University

Christopher J. Coyne
George Mason University

J. Paul Dunne
University of Cape Town

CAMBRIDGE
UNIVERSITY PRESS

CAMBRIDGE
UNIVERSITY PRESS

University Printing House, Cambridge CB2 8BS, United Kingdom

One Liberty Plaza, 20th Floor, New York, NY 10006, USA

477 Williamstown Road, Port Melbourne, VIC 3207, Australia

314–321, 3rd Floor, Plot 3, Splendor Forum, Jasola District Centre, New Delhi – 110025, India

79 Anson Road, #06–04/06, Singapore 079906

Cambridge University Press is part of the University of Cambridge.

It furthers the University's mission by disseminating knowledge in the pursuit of education, learning, and research at the highest international levels of excellence.

www.cambridge.org
Information on this title: www.cambridge.org/9781108926249
DOI: 10.1017/9781108923033

First published 2021

A catalogue record for this publication is available from the British Library.

ISBN 978-1-108-92624-9 Paperback
ISSN 2632-332X (online)
ISSN 2632-3311 (print)

The Economics of Conflict and Peace

History and Applications

Elements in Defence Economics

DOI: 10.1017/9781108923033
First published online: May 2021

Shikha Basnet Silwal
Washington and Lee University

Charles H. Anderton
College of the Holy Cross

Jurgen Brauer
Chulalongkorn University

Christopher J. Coyne
George Mason University

J. Paul Dunne
University of Cape Town

Author for correspondence: Shikha Basnet Silwal, silwals@wlu.edu

Abstract: Written for an audience of students, general readers, and economists alike, this Element is a primer on the field of the economics of conflict and peace. It offers a systematic, and detailed overview – even if in broad strokes – of the field's orthodox and heterodox history of thought and current theories and evidence. The authors view this Element as a baseline account on which to build a future, separate, and more fully developed work on the economics of peace, economic growth, and human development. Altogether, the Element contextualizes the field of conflict and peace economics, outlines its history of thought, highlights examples of current theoretical and empirical scholarship in the field, and maps trajectories for further research.

Keywords: history of thought, conflict economics, peace economics, military economics, security economics

JEL classifications: B1, D74, O1, F50, H56

ISBNs: 9781108926249 (PB), 9781108923033 (OC)
ISSNs: 2632-332X (online), 2632-3311 (print)

Contents

Introduction

Written for an audience of students, general readers, and economists alike, this volume is a primer on the field of the economics of conflict and peace. It offers a reasonably comprehensive, systematic, and detailed overview – even if in broad strokes – of the field's orthodox and heterodox history of thought and current theories and evidence. We view this Element as a baseline account on which to build a future, separate and more fully developed, piece on the economics of peace, economic growth, and human development.

In terms of process, Brauer and Silwal conceptualized the volume. Anderton, Brauer, Coyne, Dunne, and Silwal contributed draft sections, and all authors then reviewed, critiqued, and constructively commented on each other's work. Anderton and Silwal wrestled the citations and references into shape, Brauer carried out the final editing for integration, cohesion, and flow, and Silwal led the overall effort to shepherd the volume through to production. Content-wise, Section 1, written by Anderton and Brauer and the only section in Part I, situates the field of conflict and peace economics within the discipline of economics. Part II is a synopsis of the fields' intellectual history. We start in Section 2 with Coyne's introduction to the Austrian school of economics and its perhaps surprising relevance for conflict and peace economics today. Marxian, post-Keynesian, and other heterodox economists' thoughts are reviewed in Section 3, written by Dunne. Arranged by subfield, Section 4, written by Silwal with contributions by Brauer, characterizes the development of the mostly neoclassical and neo-Keynesian post-Second World War literature. From history of thought, the Element moves in Part III to presentations of selected theory and evidence of the contemporary literature. Coyne illustrates in Section 5 how preparing for and engaging in war increases the scale and scope of government in overlooked, and politically and economically often uncomfortable and crucial, ways. In a similar vein, Dunne reviews the literature on the effects of military expenditure and the cost of war on economic development in Section 6, a literature stimulated although by no means dominated by heterodox views. Rounding out Part III, Anderton and Brauer summarize examples of neoclassical-based theories and empirical case studies in Section 7. Section 8, the only section in Part IV, and written in the main by Silwal, then turns to underexplored and altogether missing topics in conflict and peace economics research.

Altogether, the Element (a) *contextualizes* the field of conflict and peace economics, (b) *outlines* its history of thought, (c) *highlights* examples of current theoretical and empirical scholarship in the field, and (d) *maps* trajectories for further research.

Part I Context and Overview

1 Conflict and Peace in Economic Perspective

Nabad iyo caano, col iyo abaar. [Peace and milk, war and famine.]

– Somali proverb

This section situates the field of conflict and peace economics within the academic discipline of economics. We begin by contextualizing conflict and economics and present four ways to think about economies and economics in relation to conflict and peace. Next, we characterize subfields within the field and discuss the interdependencies between economics and conflict, concluding with a foray into the nature of the peace and security good. The discussion provides a rich tapestry interwoven with selected examples of conflict and peace economics (theory and evidence) throughout the Element.

1.1 The Ubiquity of Conflict

Conflict is ubiquitous. Economics enters the fray because conflict invariably affects decisions regarding resource allocation and trade within and between households, within and between firms, and within and between nations.[1] A prominent contributor to the field, Jack Hirshleifer, writes of conflict examples such as "back-biting maneuvers for advancement on the promotion ladder," of "family squabbles ranging from the trivial to the deadly serious," of rival firms finding "ways of sabotaging competing enterprises," of nations "at war or else at peace," of "a trade union [which] may call a strike or else sign a collective bargaining contract," and of "a lawsuit [that] may be settled or litigated in court" (Hirshleifer 2001, p. 45). Thus viewed, one might well say that *all of economics is conflict economics*. Conflict is about diverging interests. The success or failure of conflict resolution revolves around how best to negotiate this divergence, which, in turn, depends on how to understand parties' willingness and ability to negotiate and on the many factors that impinge on this willingness and ability. Haggling over the price of vegetables at the local farmer's market, for example, is conflictual. Buyers want to pay as lttle as possible; sellers want to receive as much as possible. Sometimes conflict is over the *distribution* of goods and services produced – for instance, a disagreement in a labor dispute about how much workers should be paid as opposed to a firm's financiers. At other times, it is the productive capacity itself, the

---

[1] This section is a further development of Brauer and Anderton (2020). Literature references may be found therein.

resources with which to produce in the first place (such as land and equipment), that is in contention. Who should own, occupy, and work land and agricultural implements? *Conflict settlement*, if it occurs, may be time-limited, lasting for a period before breaking down again. Settlement can be cooperative and *voluntary* (hagglers agree on a price or else they agree not to trade at all), or it can be noncooperative and *coerced* (the vegetables are stolen, for example, or the seller surreptitiously mismeasures their weight).

War and peace, threat and defense, conflict and settlement, struggle and appeasement, production and predation, appropriation and exchange, defection and cooperation, selfishness and selflessness all point to contrasting ends of a spectrum so that if all of economics is conflict economics, then one might equally well say that *all of economics is peace economics*! For an economy even to subsist, some minimal amount of peace must be present. In the wake of the Second World War, another giant of the field, Kenneth Boulding, put it this way: "Essentially, the economic problem of reconstruction is that of rebuilding the capital of society" (Boulding 1945). Without capital, including human capital (our talent, education, skill, ingenuity, entrepreneurship, and "sweat equity"), economies can be neither constructed nor reconstructed. Although not sufficient, *peace is necessary for prosperity*, and the incorporation of conflict into economic models is an essential part of the economics discipline. Economics must study why conflict happens, how it is carried out, and what can be done to resolve, mitigate, and prevent it.

❖ Conflict is ubiquitous.
❖ All of economics is conflict economics.
❖ All of economics is peace economics.
❖ Peace is necessary for prosperity.

1.2 Thinking Economically about Conflict and Peace

1.2.1 The Four Economies

Figure 1 depicts four ways to think about economies. Box 1 of the figure refers to the *exchange economy*, which best functions in a free, private, and competitive environment. That is, exchange (trade) should be voluntary; government intrusion, save for basic rule-setting, should be absent; and buyers and sellers should be able to switch trade partners with only minimal, if any, restriction. A second economy is the *grants economy*

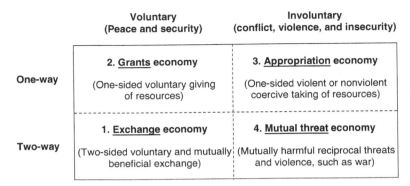

Figure 1 The four economies
Source: Adapted from Brauer and Anderton (2020, p. 444).

(Box 2 of the figure). It refers to the one-sided, self-denying, and voluntary giving away of resources (Boulding, Pfaff, and Horvath 1972). Parents give allowances to their children, people fund their favorite charities, and nation-states provide foreign aid to ease humanitarian emergencies. The third and fourth types of economies are the *appropriation economy* and the *mutual threat economy* (Boxes 3 and 4 in the figure), characterized by the threatened or actual violent appropriation of someone else's resources.

If Boxes 3 and 4 of Figure 1 reflect conflict economics, then Boxes 1 and 2 reflect peace economics. The dashed borders separating the boxes indicate that they are not mutually exclusive. The high likelihood of the one-sided taking of resources, for example, makes households, firms, and nation-states invest in defense and security. Such investment often is made through the exchange economy – for example, by purchasing an alarm system for one's home. Moreover, such investments can incentivize voluntary over involuntary trans-actions (better to trade than to steal), thus helping institutionalize the evolution of societies toward voluntary economic processes.

Most economics textbooks – even at the graduate level of study – focus to excess on the exchange economy, wholly ignoring a vast swath of economic reality. In the United States, the government's Bureau of Labor Statistics, for example, has recorded the size of nonprofit organizations' labor force at 12.5 million people in 2017 – that is, more than 8 percent of the country's total level of employment.[2]

---

[2] See www.bls.gov/bdm/nonprofits/nonprofits.htm.

1.2.2 Conflict Economics: Definition and Subfields

Within the economics profession, the fields of the *economics of crime* and *law and economics* are well-established, as is *defense economics*, but until recently it seemingly has not been well recognized that they all can be subsumed under the umbrella of *conflict economics*, which we take as the overarching name of the field. We define conflict economics as applying economic concepts, tools, and methods to the study of (1) the threat or actuality of conflict and any associated diminution or appropriation of income or assets; (2) conflict resolution, mitigation, and prevention; and (3) norm and institution building toward stable, irreversible peace. Most research in the field focuses on the first of this definition's three aspects, comparatively neglecting the others. This is not due to economists' general aversion to pronouncements on what *should* be done regarding the difficulties encountered when studying how conflicts are in fact resolved and how peace is actually achieved.[3]

> Conflict economics applies economic concepts, tools, and methods to the study of (1) the threat or actuality of conflict and any associated diminution or appropriation of income or assets; (2) conflict resolution, mitigation, and prevention; and (3) norm and institution building toward stable, irreversible peace. As such, the field broadly covers causes, conduct, and consequences of conflict.

Among those who study *violent, politically motivated conflict*, in particular, the terms *conflict, defense, security, military, war,* and *peace economics* tend to be used interchangeably, but there is some order among them. To threaten appropriation, credible force must be available to carry out or defend against the threat. This implies funding the necessary labor and equipment, such as soldiers and weapons. *Military economics* focuses on the opportunity cost of this funding (that is, what else these resources could have bought). While prominent by the 1980s, military economics arose much earlier in the Austrian school of economics and in class struggle–oriented, Marxian-inspired works on capitalism and imperialism,

---

[3] Exceptions notwithstanding, economics is a descriptive rather than a normative science. It studies *what is* rather than what one wishes *should be* the case. At least two caveats emerge: If free, voluntary, noncoerced trade *is* mutually beneficial (descriptive), then governments *should not* inhibit or restrict trade (normative). This is an example of an implicit *norm of economic efficiency* that the discipline's preeminent neoclassical approach upholds – a norm not all people will want to agree to. Other theoretical approaches feature their own implicit norms. The other caveat is this: if norms contribute to what society *is* at the present moment (for example, a norm that relegates women to intra-household work), then economics must of course study these norms as part of its descriptive effort to understand and explain that which is. Studying norms is not necessarily at odds with economics.

extending, for example, into dependency theory in the field of development economics (see Sections 2 and 3). Today, however, this subfield often is presented in neoclassical, post-Keynesian, and neo-Keynesian terms and tends to focus more narrowly on the economy-wide opportunity cost of military expenditure or on government budgetary trade-offs between military and other types of spending (see Section 6). The subfield has evolved in this way partly as an outward-looking response, beyond the defense sector, to what had been the generally inward-looking *defense economics* of the 1960s. Initially covering topics such as defense budget management, manpower recruitment, defense procurement, nuclear threat postures, and free-riding behavior in defense alliances such as the North Atlantic Treaty Organization (NATO), the subfield of defense economics has since broadened to include topics such as arms production and trade, arms trade offset deals and dual-use technology, arms rivalries and arms control, and disarmament and peacekeeping (Section 4).

Distinctly discernable but not quite as prominent is the field's extension into public sector *security economics* more generally, especially since September 11, 2001 (henceforth referred to as 9/11). Security economics is concerned with intelligence services, espionage and cybersecurity, homeland security (including terrorism, counterterrorism, and defense against criminal syndicates), and the security of public infrastructure, utilities, and other assets. It thus blends into the *economics of crime*. The private sector, likewise, faces numerous security concerns and often addresses them through the exchange economy with the acquisition of goods such as perimeter fences, security cameras, and the employment of large numbers of security guards at schools, workplaces, and entertainment venues. Much of this reflects households' and firms' attempts to address risk. Security economics blends into the *economics of insurance* and might expand to include risks related to bioeconomics such as natural disasters, climate change threats, and pandemics. In time, conflict economics may become broader than even Hirshleifer (2001) anticipated: it might come to cover the whole of human safety and security, public and private.

War economics emerged with the growing anticipation of what became the First World War and dealt with the conduct and consequences of state-on-state warfare in Europe, as well as the subsequent postwar resource reconversion and economic reconstruction.[4] Much of the debate dealt with frictions in international trade and finance resulting from countries' mercantilist policy postures. As such, war economics also studied the causes of war, and this international context influenced topics studied by the Austrian school and Marxian

---

[4] See Anderton and Anderton (1997), Anderton (2003), Coulomb (2004), and Brauer (2017) for coverage of notable early economists such as Edgeworth, Keynes, Pigou, Robbins, Veblen, Wicksell, and others.

economics, indeed by Adam Smith himself. A *conflict economics* narrower than Hirshleifer's conception began when economists and quantitative political scientists joined to study an explosion of intrastate wars observed since the mid- to late 1970s. The concern here lay with the possibility of the de-development of postcolonial developing economies due to large-scale, widespread, and persistent violence. In focusing on the causes, conduct, and consequences of intrastate war, it somewhat neglected peace itself, and this is where *peace economics* enters. More explicitly interested in conflict resolution, mitigation, and prevention than any of the other subfields, peace economics ultimately asks questions about the existence and stability of the social contracts between and among populations and, as such, is tied to bargaining theory (as exemplified in Thomas Schelling's 1960 work *The Strategy of Conflict*), to aspects of political economy and constitutional law, and to the economics of such law, as well as to broader norm and institution building for peace (see Section 8).

1.2.3 Interdependencies between Conflict and Economics

Figure 2 indicates some ways in which economics and violent conflict are related. Box 1 highlights that prior to acting, decision makers first have to *decide* on an action – to decide literally means "to cut away." What is cut away is a set of alternatives. To decide is to exercise *choice*. Economists' choice theoretic models thus can be applied to choices for war or peace, choices about whether to intervene in a conflict, and even the choice to engage in mass atrocities such as genocide (see Section 7). As shown in the sub-box, making such choices involves both the rational weighing of costs and benefits and nonrational elements, the latter gleaned from the intersections of psychology, sociology, and anthropology with economics.

Conflict is a choice. Economists' choice-theoretic models can thus be applied to allegedly noneconomic contexts.

Box 2 states that economic conditions can affect aspects such as the onset risk, duration, seriousness, termination, and recurrence of violent conflict. Conversely, economic conditions can affect the likelihood that *non*violent approaches are pursued, along with whether or not fragile peace can be reinforced and moved toward stable peace. Box 3 states that conflict affects economic outcomes. The "5 Ds" in the sub-box stand, first, for *disruption* – for example, war's disruption of education, trade, and economic growth. The second D, for *diversion*, refers to the shifting of resources from civilian-oriented investment toward supporting a war economy. Next are the costs

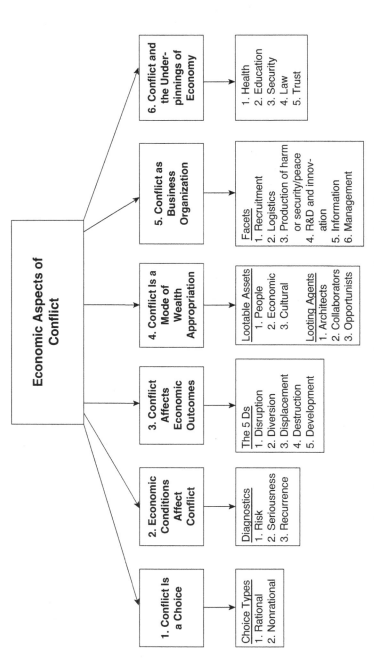

Figure 2 Interdependences between economics and conflict

Source: Adapted from Anderton and Brauer (2016a, p. 6).

associated with *displacement* of people (refugees) and of capital (capital flight) or, worse, their *destruction* (including of our natural environment; i.e., ecological resources), followed, lastly, by postwar (re)*development difficulties*, all themes variously taken up in the following sections. Not shown but implied are the at times substantial investment costs of conflict intervention and peacekeeping, of peacebuilding and conflict resolution (conflict settlement), of subsequent disarmament and demobilization, and of the general peace and security benefits of peace promotion.

Box 4 acknowledges that conflict can be a mode of wealth acquisition, and the sub-box suggests that examples of lootable assets include people (e.g., human trafficking, child soldiers), economic assets (land, minerals), and cultural assets (a people-group's social bonds, artifacts, history, language, and very existence). Standard, exchange economy–oriented textbooks wrongly assume that production, trade, and wealth accumulation are wholly peaceful activities; in contrast, conflict economics recognizes, models, and integrates appropriation possibilities into the standard models. Recognizing conflict as a mode of wealth acquisition directly leads to Box 5, which emphasizes that war or other forms of conflict involve a variety of organizational or business-related practices. The listed items suggest that fields such as industrial organization and management science may have much to offer to conflict economics to offer more insight into how (threatened) violence is planned and carried out or how those working on peace promotion can improve upon their countervailing efforts.

Finally, Box 6 points to the societal underpinnings of an economy. Those seeking violence often undermine key facets of their own and rivals' economies, while peacebuilders typically work to sustain or rebuild them. That "man doth not live by bread only" (Deuteronomy 8:3) was known to ancient peoples, and economists likewise long ago acknowledged economies' reliance on broader political and cultural contexts. For example, in his *Political Economy* text, published in 1850, Nassau W. Senior repeatedly states that "security . . . is the most important of all services" that government can supply.[5]

1.2.4 The Nature of the Peace and Security Good

Standard economics characterizes national defense as a pure *public good*. Once provided, it is not feasible to exclude, for instance, nontaxpayers from whatever security services national defense offers (defense is a nonexcludable service, it is said). Additionally, national defense benefits multitudes of people at the same

---

[5] An online copy of Nassau's 1854 third edition is available at www.econlib.org/library/Senior/snP .html.

time (it is nonrivalous). In practice, however, the nature of peace and security goods is more varied than that. For example, a private security company may be hired to safeguard shipments sent by a relief organization to assist in humanitarian emergencies. Here, security is a *private good* (rival and excludable). A defense alliance such as NATO is a *club good* (all paid-up members benefit in a nonrival manner and nonpayers are excluded). And, in some cases, ostensibly widely available protection is in fact restricted to a limited number of beneficiaries, a *common resource-pool good*. For example, an aircraft's emergency exit doors cover all passengers (nonexcludable), but competition (rivalry) is fierce when the need for their use arises. With limited exceptions (e.g., Todd Sandler and colleagues), conflict economics as a whole tends to discuss defense, security, and peace as unitary pure public goods when it is more likely that their economic nature morphs across space, time, and circumstances.

We additionally highlight an observation made by Sandler (1999). In the peace and security context, standard theory fails to acknowledge two important assumptions – namely, that national defense, for example, is provided (1) only for the current generation and (2) only over a well-defined national territory. If decision makers were less myopic and also accounted for *future* generations of residents (a transgenerational good), then the sum of benefits would be larger, warranting a larger expense. Similarly, decision makers can ignore future generations but instead consider residents in allied territories (a transboundary good). Relative to myopic awareness, the larger benefit to be gained justifies a larger cost to be borne. Finally, one can consider the benefit across all territories and across all future generations. This benefit is larger still, justifying considerable security costs to be carried. We call this enlightened policy stance *the Buddha rule*. What Sandler highlights, moreover, is that a solution to a current-day transboundary problem may pose a future transgenerational one. More broadly, intragenerational dispute settlement may stoke conflict a generation later as, for instance, Keynes warned in his *The Economic Consequences of the Peace* (1919) would happen if Germany were held to what he strenuously argued were the Treaty of Versailles' onerous provisions. Sadly, his warning was not heeded.

Having set out the context of conflict and peace economics within the economics discipline as a whole, the next three sections provide a brief intellectual history of the subfield.

Part II   A Short History of Thought
2 The Austrian School: Insights on the War Economy

Following an introduction to the Austrian school of economics, this section presents insights from core contributions of subsequent generations of Austrian school scholars with an emphasis on their relevance for understanding conflict and peace economics. This includes enhancing our understanding of the nature of the war economy, appreciating the opportunity cost of physical and human capital used in conflict, identifying various channels through which war can undermine economic growth, and understanding the role of economic exchange for sustained peace.

2.1 Foundation: Carl Menger's *Principles of Economics*

The Austrian school of economics dates back to the publication of Carl Menger's *Principles of Economics* (1871). Menger, in the Austrian Empire (hence the Austrian school), was one of the three cofounders of the "marginal revolution" in economics, along with Léon Walras, a Frenchmen then teaching at the University of Lausanne, Switzerland, and William Stanley Jevons, in England.[6] As a fundamental paradigm shift in the foundations of economic analysis, from the labor theory of value (discussed in Section 3) to the marginal utility theory of value, this revolution is central to the study of economics today. As it turns out, the concepts developed in Menger's *Principles* also apply to the study of war.

Menger's *Principles* developed concepts that are central to the study of economics and the study of war.

In his opening section, Menger delineates four defining features of a good. First, there must be a human want that requires satisfaction. Second, the item must be able to satisfy this need. Third, people must possess knowledge of the ability of the item to satisfy their needs. Finally, actors must possess command over the good to use it to satisfy their wants. An economic good, as Menger defines it, is a good that is scarce – meaning it is not freely available in sufficient quantities to satisfy all peoples' wants. Economic goods are subject to economizing activity, meaning that people need to make (marginal) decisions about how to allocate scarce resources among competing alternatives.

Menger next develops a theory of value grounded in subjectivism and marginalism. The value of a good, he argues, is determined by how people perceive the usefulness of an additional (marginal) unit of the good for fulfilling their needs. Value is not something inherent in goods but is a function of a good's perceived ability to satisfy a want. Menger presents a taxonomy of where goods fit into the structure of producing final consumer goods. "Higher-order" goods are inputs

---

[6] Léon Walras published *Éléments d'économie politique pure* in 1874. The first English translation, by William Jaffé, published in 1954, was of Walras's fifth edition (*Elements of Pure Economics*, London, Allen & Unwin). William Stanley Jevons published *The Theory of Political Economy* in 1871. See also Jevons (1866).

into producing "lower-order" goods, which ultimately produce final consumer goods (goods of the "first order"). Consider a computer. Raw materials would be goods of the highest order, and internal elements produced with these raw materials would be lower-order goods. The completed computer would be a first-order good. This taxonomy is important for two reasons. First, it underpins the idea of derived demand – the value of higher-order goods is derived from its usefulness in producing a first-order good valued by consumers. Second, this taxonomy is at the foundation of capital theory. Production entails a sequential process in which capital goods are transformed into final consumer goods. The process is complicated in that capital goods are both heterogeneous (each physic-ally unique) and multi-specific (they have numerous potential uses; Böhm-Bawerk 1889, Lachmann 1956). This means that decisions need to be made about how to combine scarce capital goods to produce value-added outputs from an array of possible uses and combinations.[7]

Finally, Menger develops a theory of exchange and price. Exchange takes place under three conditions. First, people must place different values on the goods they possess versus the goods other people own. In order to engage in exchange, you must value what I own more than what you possess and vice versa. Absent these different valuations, there would be no grounds for exchange. Second, people must know about the trading opportunity. Third, people must have the ability to engage in the exchange. Prices emerge out of the process of exchange and reflect the quantities of goods exchanged based on the subjective valuations of market participants. To see how Menger's ideas are relevant to understanding the eco-nomics of conflict, it is necessary to first consider two contrasting views of the war economy held by economists in the early 1900s.[8]

2.2 Two Views on the War Economy

In 1919, Otto Neurath published an article, "Through War Economy to Economy in Kind," which pointed to the effectiveness of central economic planning by European governments during the First World War. Noting the precision and coordination of deliberate social planning involved in the war economy, which effectively achieved war-related objectives while increasing employment and

---

[7] Influenced by Menger, Eugen von Böhm-Bawerk would develop Menger's theory of capital in theoretical detail. Interestingly, Böhm-Bawerk worked both as a professor of economics and as Austria's Minster of Finance during three different appointments over the 1895–1904 period. A proponent of sound money and fiscal responsibility, he resigned from his position as Minister of Finance in 1904 due to military-related pressures on the budget that he viewed as irresponsible and dangerous.

[8] For detail and context on the relevance of Austrian economics for understanding defense, peace, conflict, and war economics, see Kjar and Anderson (2010); Westley, Anderson, and Kjar (2011); Anderson, Kjar, and Yohe (2012); and Coyne (2020).

minimizing economic fluctuations, the experience demonstrated in Neurath's view that a large-scale centrally planned economy could successfully operate and should be extended to peacetime. Neurath's plan for extending the war economy included abolishing money and establishing a "central office for measurement in kind" that would use nonmonetary statistics to plan economic activity as if the economy were one large enterprise (Neurath 1919, p. 141). Under his proposed system, "production and consumption are brought closer together, and objects and men present themselves in a more flexible way. The veiling concealments produced by 'currency', 'exchange rate', 'boom', 'depression', etc., are suddenly removed. Everything becomes transparent and controllable." Extending the administrative state of the war economy to all economic activity would, in Neurath's estimation, significantly improve human welfare.

> Neurath's and Mises's contrasting visions of central planning were the basis for the socialist calculation debate, which is central to understanding what the war economy can and cannot achieve.

In that same year, Ludwig von Mises published *Nation, State, and Economy*. Writing in the wake of the Central Power's defeat, Mises explored the nature of the war economy, noting that all resources "had to be regarded as a mass under the control of a unified administration that could be drawn on for equally meeting the needs of all, and so consumption had to be rationed" (1919, p. 118). Political decision-making curtailed, or completely replaced, individual decision-making in private markets, he argued. He further contended that the war economy threatened the widespread prosperity generated by markets by distorting, or eliminating, market prices and profit and loss, which are central to the entrepreneurial market process necessary to allocate scarce resources to satisfy consumer's wants.

Neurath and Mises laid out two quite different visions of the war economy. For Neurath, the war economy was a model for centrally planning the entire economy to improve human well-being. In his view, expert planning would replace the anarchy of the market economy and in the process significantly improve the welfare of the citizenry. For Mises, in contrast, extending the methods used in the war economy threatened the dynamism of markets and posed a threat to human well-being. These contrasting visions of central planning were the basis of the socialist calculation debate, which is central to understanding what the war economy can and cannot achieve.

2.3 The Calculation Debate

Similar to Neurath, early advocates of socialism argued that it was possible to rationalize economic production by abolishing both private property rights over the means of production and money while centralizing economic production in the hands of a central planning board. Mises (1920, 1922, 1949) argued that the means proposed by the socialists were not conducive to achieving their goal of advanced material production. Nationalizing the means of production would destroy the mechanisms necessary for the operation of the entrepreneurial process.

Building on Menger's theory of exchange and the emergence of prices, Mises argued that in the absence of property rights over the means of production, there could be no exchange and, hence, no market prices. Absent market prices, there would be no way for economic planners to engage in economic calculation, which refers to the ability to judge the expected value added of alternative uses of scarce resources. Mises's general point was that there would be no way for planners to solve the economic problem of determining how to allocate scarce resources across a range of technologically feasible alternatives. From an economic standpoint, there is a fundamental difference between efforts to satisfy a single hierarchy of ends – for example, building more bombs, tanks, guns, and so on – determined by war planners and discovering how to allocate, and reallocate, scarce resources across all possible uses to satisfy consumer wants, which are constantly evolving. The former characterizes the war economy, while the latter characterizes the market process.

Advocates of socialism revised their models to incorporate Mises's critique resulting in the "market socialism" model proposed by Abba Lerner (1934, 1936, 1937, 1938) and Oskar Lange (1936, 1937). Market socialism allowed for money and market exchange in final consumer goods and labor markets but maintained the nationalization of the means of production under the control of a Central Planning Board (CPB). The CPB would provide provisional prices for inputs to firms and instruct them to follow the strictures of the perfectly competitive market model by setting a price equal to the marginal cost of production while producing the level of output that minimized average costs. Moreover, the CPB would adjust provisional prices as necessary by responding to surpluses (by reducing prices) and shortages (by increasing prices), just as firms do in competitive markets.

At this point, Mises's Viennese colleague, F. A. Hayek (1945, pp. 119–208), responded to the market socialists, arguing that they had failed to provide a solution to the calculation problem. Their proposed solution assumed what it needed to demonstrate. While it was indeed true that mimicking the perfectly competitive model would lead to efficiency, this assumed that the knowledge embedded in the model – that is, the cost curves, which include not only explicit costs but also opportunity costs – were known, ex ante, to producers. Hayek argued that markets allow entrepreneurs to continually discover the relevant economic knowledge – consumer wants, economic costs, new and more efficient production methods, and new products and services – that emerges through the process of interaction and experimentation. This knowledge does not exist absent the market process that allows for its emergence.

2.4 Implications for Understanding the War Economy, Past and Future

The calculation debate offers insight into the *economic* nature of the war economy. War production requires the diversion of resources from private uses, redirected either into the exclusive control of war planners in the administrative state or else redirected into hybrid public-private arrangements where the administrative state interacts with private producers to achieve the predetermined ends of war planners. In both cases, it is possible to produce predetermined, war-related outputs, which is a purely technological issue, but not for planners to solve the economic problem.

> The calculation debate offers insight into the economic nature of the war economy.

As Hayek (1945, pp. 77–8) emphasized, the core economic problem is

> not merely a problem of how to allocate "given" resources – if "given" is taken to mean given to a single mind which deliberately solves the problem set by these "data." It is rather a problem of how to secure the best use of resources known to any of the members of society, for ends whose relative importance only these individuals know.

Increasing war production does increase overall outputs, but that is different from using scarce resources to fulfill the wants of individual members of society.

To clarify this point, consider a cartoon first published in *Krokodil*, a satirical Soviet magazine. The cartoon shows two Soviet factory workers standing under a one-ton nail hoisted above them. One worker asks, "Who needs a one-ton nail?" The other replies, "Who cares? The important thing is that we fulfilled the plan for nails in one fell swoop!" (quoted in Gray 1990, p. 9). In meeting planners' predetermined production targets, the factory has indeed increased total output. But in doing so, the scarce resources used to increase output contributed nothing to improving the well-being of citizens who have no use for a one-ton nail. This same logic illustrates the operation of the war economy, as resources are employed and output increases, but there is no clear mechanism to provide the knowledge and incentives to ensure improvements in the welfare of the populace.

There are two areas where this insight tends to be neglected. First is the belief that war production contributes to increases in well-being, as reflected in aggregate macroeconomic measures such as output, employment, and spending. This, however, confuses increases in output, which requires dedicating more resources to producing more predetermined goods, with improvement in economic well-being, which requires using scarce resources to produce outputs *valued by consumers*. An example will illustrate this confusion. Many believe that the Second World War was a source of prosperity in the United States. The evidence offered for this belief is decreased unemployment, increases in output, and increases in consumption during the war effort. Economic historian Robert Higgs (2006, pp. 61–80), drawing on insights by Mises and Hayek, reconsiders the data and concludes that the prosperity associated with the Second World War is misunderstood. According to official statistics, unemployment dropped during the war. But this was the result of increased employment in the military sector, which did not contribute to producing consumer goods. As Higgs writes, "the 'prosperous' condition of the labor force was spurious: Official unemployment was virtually nonexistent, but four-tenths of the total labor force was not being used to produce consumer goods or capital comparable of yielding consumer goods in the future" (2006, pp. 63–4). Military conscription or government-subsidized employment producing military-related outputs is not the same as being employed in the private sector to produce outputs to satiate consumer wants. Aggregate employment statistics mask this reality by treating all employment as equal in terms of the economic value added. From this perspective, employment to produce a bomb is the equivalent of employment to produce food. But from the perspective of individual well-being, which is what prosperity is about, these things are quite different.

What about gross national product (GNP), which increased during the war? Higgs argues that the aggregate measure masks the specifics of what output was produced as part of the war effort. As illustrated by the one-ton nail, there is a difference between producing outputs that improve the well-being of private consumers and outputs that satisfy war-planner targets. In private markets, the value that consumers place on output is indicated by the market prices, which, as Menger, Mises, and Hayek emphasized, emerges through voluntary exchange. In wartime production, in contrast, prices are not determined in competitive markets but instead are negotiated through a series of contracts facilitated through bureaucratic rules. The result is that government spending on military goods captures costs and not consumer value as in markets. When Higgs removes military-related expenditures from the GNP data, he finds that output fell during the 1942–4 period (2006, pp. 65–7).[9]

What about consumption? Adjusting consumption figures to account for inflation, which reduces the purchasing power of consumers, Higgs (2006, p. 70) finds that "real consumption per capita reached a prewar peak in 1941 that was nearly 9 percent above the 1939 level; it declined by more than 6 percent during 1941–3 and rose during 1943–5; still, even in 1945, it had not recovered to the 1941 level." Beyond aggregate consumption measures, consumers also incurred the cost of price controls and wartime rationing imposed by the government as part of the wartime effort. Together, this counters the standard orthodoxy that real consumption increased during the war.

A second area where the insights of the calculation debate tend to be overlooked relates to wartime innovation. Innovations produced by war-related spending are often believed to have significant spillovers to civilian life. Examples include the internet, GPS, software, and nuclear power (see Ruttan 2006 and Brauer 2007a, 2007b for discussion). That war-related research generates some innovations and spillovers is not surprising. However, from an economic standpoint, the issue is not that war-related research can generate spillover benefits, but instead the opportunity cost of the resources employed in generating those benefits.

Opportunity cost is important in two contexts. First, even when focusing on cases of successful innovation, what were the opportunity costs? What could have been produced if the employed resources had been devoted to alternative uses? Second, an accurate economic accounting requires us to also account for instances of innovation failures. Many focus purely on cases of *successful* innovation and then use those instances as evidence of the overall success of military-related research (Coyne and Bradley 2019, pp. 222–4; Coyne 2020, pp. 28–9). What matters, moreover, is the institutional environment allowing for the emergence of the economic knowledge and means for sorting among the array of possible uses of scarce resources. The issue is that there is no way for military planners to gauge the opportunity cost of resources absent economic calculation and, therefore, no way to make net welfare claims regarding the value added of resources in military-related research (Coyne and Bills 2018).

The insights of Austrian school scholars on the war economy remain relevant today.

---

[9] According to another analysis, "in 1941, government spending represented approximately 30% of GDP, or almost US$408 billion. At its peak in 1944, this had risen to over US$1.6 trillion or 79% of total GDP rising by 394% in just three years. By contrast, consumption fell from 67% to 46% of GDP and investment fell from 11% to 3% of GDP over the same period" (Institute for Economics and Peace 2011, p. 7).

The insights of Austrian scholars on the war economy remain relevant today because they focus on the epistemic (knowledge) aspects of the economic problem and the institutional environment necessary to discover the answer to that problem. They also demonstrate the applicability and importance of core economic concepts – opportunity cost, marginalism, subjective valuation, and choice – to matters of war production and the implications for human welfare.

The next two sections discuss other economic schools of thought. Like the Austrians, these, too, often have taken issue with militarism and war as important economic concerns.

3 Marxian and Heterodox Views

This section outlines contributions by heterodox economists on the understanding of conflict, war, and peace. The Marxist tradition sees military expenditure and war as possibly economically damaging, but of necessity for capitalism. The section also reviews the subsequent development of naïve military Keynesianism. Institutionalist perspectives are also touched on, which, akin to the Austrian school (Section 2), posit for instance the existence of a military-industrial complex (MIC) that creates domestic pressure to increase military expenditure independent of threats, with ensuing economic inefficiencies.

3.1 Context

Historically, economists considered the role of security and defense as fundamental concerns. Viewing global wealth as a fixed quantity, mercantilists saw its pursuit as a zero-sum game requiring nation-state competition to obtain desired shares of the economic cake. To prosper, back then in the form of gold, they championed exports (gold coming in) while limiting imports (gold going out). This inspired violent conflict and imperialism as major powers fought over international export markets. Indeed, Thomas Hobbes's political theory spelled out in *Leviathan* (1651) had argued that a nation's survival in an anarchic world would depend upon its dealing with a permanent state of war. So, governments needed to regulate the national economy to gain state power at the expense of rivals. Defense and offense were seen as *inherent and foundational* to the international economy, with peace only maintained when a hegemon (superpower) existed to dominate. Following Adam Smith's *Wealth of Nations* (1776), an alternative perspective was developed: trade was not a zero-sum game. Freely trading states could increase mutual wealth rather than share a fixed sum thereof. Immanuel Kant also argued, in *Perpetual Peace* (1795), that free trade could create wealth for all and bring global peace and civilizational progress. War was a costly mistake in that it damaged trade and would lead to a burden of debt if financed by loans. Wars could not be justified by benefits of predation and territorial gains and, at least, could only be a temporary phenomenon. Later, Vilfredo Pareto's *Cours d'économie politique* (vol. I, 1896; vol. II, 1897) denounced war as being of no value, arguing that it merely reflected governments' use of external threats to increase internal control, ensure social cohesion, and cover up corruption.[10] And just prior to the First World War, Norman Angell's *The Great Illusion* (1910) made an influential argument that the supposed benefits of war were an illusion.[11] This section places Marxian work into this context of nation-state, war, and economy.

3.2 Marxian Perspectives

3.2.1 Theoretical Aspects

Marx was concerned with conflict – but mainly class war. He had planned to write a volume of *Capital* on the state, which would have dealt with military and civil industry and international relations. Though it was never completed, it was to argue that national conflicts and crises could encourage the search for external markets and that this economic conflict, in turn, could lead to military conflict (Coulomb 2004). In his collaboration with Marx, Engels provided most of the specialist writing, with his main statement in *Anti-Dühring* (1878) influenced by military theorist Clausewitz, who had argued that wars were simply an extension of politics. For Engels, wars were won by technology, but this led to ruinous arms races. For Marx and Engels, the implied military expenditure would have negative effects, but there was the possibility that it could play other roles in supporting capitalism. Recently, Streeck (2020) has made a convincing case that Engel's analysis of the development of the means of destruction alongside the means of production, with a central role for technology, provided an important understanding of the rising power and independent agency of the state. The increasing threat of other industrial states could be used by ruling elites to block the path of class war through appeals to national interest. This could well lead to actual war. In this way, Engels foresaw the nature and destruction of the First World War.

Marx's method and analysis allowed his followers to develop theories of imperialism that explained war as resulting from the competition for foreign markets and an understanding of the role of militarism within capitalist economies.

---

[10] Pareto had succeeded Walras as chair of Political Economy at the University of Lausanne in 1893 and amplified the latter's marginal and mathematical approach to economics.

[11] These perspectives still exist in the field of international relations, from *neo-mercantilists* to *liberal realist* (or *rationalist*) views to the *idealist* perspective (see Coulomb and Dunne 2008).

Marx's analysis allowed his followers to develop theories of imperialism that explained war as resulting from competition for foreign markets and an understanding of militarism's role within capitalist economies. Marx argued that routine cyclical downturns, financial collapse, and long development waves all were the result of a dynamic system that had little in the way of checks and balances. Crises happened when goods that had been produced did not sell (realization crises), when wages were too low to provide sufficient demand (underconsumption crises), when industrial disputes arose over wages and working conditions, and when disproportionalities in the system emerged as a result of capitalism being anarchic and unregulated.

Behind this lay a *tendency* for the rate of profit to fall. Using the labor theory of value, the rate of profit declines because productivity increases reduce the amount of labor required per commodity unit produced. For Marx, profit is the surplus value (S) created during production, which is the value accruing to capital owners after labor and capital use are accounted for. The capitalist gets this surplus simply by owning the means of production while workers, bereft of options, are obliged to sell their labor power to the capitalist, who thus gets control of their labor. The *rate* of profit then is this surplus value as a share of the sum of constant capital (C) plus variable capital (V; i.e., labor). In symbols, $\Pi = S / (C + V)$. Dividing the two right-hand-side elements of the expression by V gives $\Pi = (S/V) / [(C/V) + 1]$, showing that the rate of profit on the left equals the rate of surplus value (surplus value as a share of variable capital) relative to one plus C/V. The latter ratio, C/V, is referred to as the organic composition of capital (OCC), the ratio of constant to variable capital. Rewritten for conciseness as $\Pi = e / (OCC + 1)$, the rate of profit then is the rate of exploitation e (an alternative name for the rate of surplus value), divided by the OCC plus one. Crucial to Marx's analysis now is that the OCC rises over time as a result of productivity growth – that is, ever more equipment per worker. And that implies that the profit rate *must* fall in value terms – there is nothing optional about it – so long as the exploitation rate, e, is relatively constant over time (certainly relative to OCC).

This amounted not to an immutable "law of a falling rate of profit" but rather to a law of the *tendency* for the rate of profit to fall. Marx's dialectical method of analysis well-recognized the existence of countertendencies that could temporarily operate to increase the profit rate. Certainly, he acknowledged that the rate of labor exploitation could rise; that constant capital could become cheaper through increased productivity in the sectors supplying machinery, raw materials, and intermediate products; and that expansion into markets with lower OCCs could take place. Marx, therefore, expected to see capitalism undergoing periodic crises as the forces of production changed, leading to a need for changes in the relations of production as well. The resulting class struggle between labor and capitalists could then lead to conflict and violence. Militarism was identified as one of the potential countertendencies. Military expenditure, for example, could act to support capitalism, working to keep profits from falling by keeping labor under capitalists' knell and providing demand to deal with realization and under-consumption crises.

It is worth noting that the first volume of Marx's main work, *Das Kapital*, appeared in 1867, just four years prior to Menger's *Principles*, which was to champion a very different view of value.

3.2.2 Imperialism

While Marx, who died in 1883, recognized capitalism's inherent need for continuous expansion – first taking over markets domestically and then inter-nationally, always seeking new areas where it was not yet established and where profit rates were higher – the idea was only fleshed out and debated in the 1900s and 1910s. Especially prominent were Rudolf Hilferding's *Finance Capital* (1910), Rosa Luxemburg's *The Accumulation of Capital* (1913), Karl Kautsky's article "Der Imperialismus" (1914), Nikolai Bukharin's *Imperialism and the World Economy* (1917), and Lenin's *Imperialism, the Highest Stage of Capitalism* (1919). Hilferding identified the growing importance of joint-stock companies, with their numerous, semi-anonymous shareholders taking the place of identifiable, singular capitalists. Reorganized capital increased its potential for growth, true, but also allowed for concentrated ownership – the rise of monopoly power – through buyouts and with economic sectors gradually being brought under the final control of finance capital. Banks and international finance thus assumed an important role in the analysis. Harnessed onto monop-oly capital's need for expansion, states were pressed to increase militarized expansion to secure protected colonial markets on behalf of domestic capitalist interests. Unlike Marx, however, Hilferding believed that capital concentration could be a system-stabilizing force, at least in theory. As a foremost theoretician of Germany's Social Democratic Party, his views were influential, and he rose in prominence to take brief stints as Germany's finance minister in 1923 and again from 1928–9. In espousing his Austro-Marxian views (he was Viennese by birth), he frequently clashed with Eugen von Böhm-Bawerk, the Austrian school's chief defender at the time, and also a former finance minister (see Howard and King 1989).

Rosa Luxemburg (1913), while also taking an underconsumptionist view, argued that capitalism's need to off-load surplus commodities via imperialism led to the domination by strong states of weaker states in the world system. Even if capital were to be a stabilizing force, this was no good thing for those on the receiving end. For context, recall the infamous Berlin Conference of 1884, which "regularized" the invasion, occupation, division, and colonization of Africa, almost 90 percent of which was under European control by 1890. As the world is a closed system, capitalism ultimately would break down, Luxemburg saw, but cause much harm in noncapitalist societies in the meantime. For instance, from 1904 to 1908, Germany conducted a genocide in its colony of German South West Africa, today's Namibia.

Taking a different tack, Kautsky (1914) argued that the only way to end colonists' mutually destructive wars over colonies fueled by capital's need to expand (his article appeared just two months into the onset of the First World War) was for the dominant states to agree on the equivalent of a stable banking cartel that would limit competition. Like Hilferding, he thought that capitalism could survive without militarism and war – that a peaceful capitalism was possible.[12] That view was ridiculed by Bukharin (1917) and Lenin (1919): Why would one believe that a cabal of "state capitalist trusts," aggregated into a "universal world trust," would not, like any cartel, eventually break down? They developed a pseudo-mercantilist theory of imperialism, in which imperial wars were inevitably necessary and which in time would mark the end of the capitalist mode of production.

The debate started among Menger and Marx and, joined by the German historical school (starring illustrious names such as Gustav von Schmoller, Max Weber, and Joseph Schumpeter), spread across Europe's broader intellectual landscape, taking place in the roughly sixty years between 1871 and the early 1930s. The Franko-Prussian War had run its brief course in 1871, the year in which Germany became a unified nation-state under Bismarck. European powers competed over colonial territories worldwide, with conflict-related consequences that last to this day (for example, in the ever-unsettled Middle East and North Africa region). Eventually drawing in the United States, the Great War tore the continent apart from 1914 to 1918, and the Russian revolution and civil war roiled the East from 1917 to 1923. The Great Depression followed, with Stalin and Hitler rising to totalitarian power, culminating in another world war. War and economy could not be separated, and their relation to each needed to be understood. The literature arising throughout this period is the one we thus labeled in Section 1 as *war economics*.

---

[12] Kautsky also recognized colonialism's contradictory role in capitalism: boosting demand by expanding markets under states' protective connivance does benefit capitalists, but if this is funded by taxes on profits, capitalists will resist.

3.3 Radical Political Economy

The debate continued after the Second World War. An important concern for Marxists was not only why capitalism had managed to survive the war but also why it thrived thereafter, at least until the 1970s. Some Marxist economists defended the idea of a positive impact of military expenditure on the capitalist system, presenting militarism, as Hilferding and Kautsky before them, as a factor in the stabilization of capitalism. In the United States, Paul A. Baran and Paul Sweezy's *Monopoly Capital* (1966), for example, saw military expenditure as important in preventing realization crises through the absorption of surplus without raising wages or capital. Other government expenditures could not do this, as it would add to productive capacity. Michael Kidron offered an alternative focused on commodity overproduction. He saw military expenditure as diverting capital from accumulation by creating "A Permanent Arms Economy," the title of an influential article published in 1967. For him, overproduction and unemployment had been contained in the 1950s and 1960s thanks to a high level of military expenditure, which prevented overinvestment and generated technological spillovers to the civil sector, while also favoring exports. Military expenditure slowed down economic growth by inducing a high level of profit tax and with the side effect of simultaneously slowing down the growth of the organic composition of capital in civil activities by diverting resources that could have been used for productive investments.

> As for the Austrian school, we see among Marxist economists an abiding and gradually increasing interest to come to grips not only with the entanglement of militarism, colonialism, and war, but also with nonwar militarism and the growing economic role and heft of central governments since the Second World War.

As with the Austrian school, Marxian economists had an abiding interest to come to grips not only with the entanglement of militarism, colonialism, and war – all pre–Second World War concerns – but also with nonwar militarism and the ever-growing role and heft of central governments in postwar economies. Primarily Eurocentric in outlook, postwar Marxists saw capitalism as leading to economic development, implying that it also encouraged economic development on the world stage. It became clear, however, that the West was developing rather more rapidly than did the rest of the world. While Baran (1957) introduced the ideas of backwardness and underdevelopment into Marxian analysis, identifying the existence of a center and periphery and arguing that capitalism was instead leading to underdevelopment, the point was brought to prominence by Andre

Gunder Frank's 1969 book *Latin America: Underdevelopment or Revolution.* Only partially Marxian in outlook, it carried the subtitle *Essays on the Development of Underdevelopment and the Immediate Enemy,* a theme later developed by Wallerstein, Amin, the unequal exchange theory of Emmanuel, and by world-systems theorists. Laclau, Brenner, and Warren provided critical perspectives (see Howard and King 1992, Brewer 2002).

As a matter of the history of thought of modern *development economics,* as well as of conflict and peace economics, it is important to recall that the 1950–70s period was an era during which overt colonial bonds were finally thrown off. Liberation struggles abounded and the Third World came into its own, even as the First and Second Worlds (West and East) sought to establish neocolonial beachheads in Asia, Africa, Latin America, and the Caribbean. The Belgian, British, Dutch, French, and Portuguese colonial empires all collapsed, often violently. Military or otherwise despotic dictatorships frequently arose in their place, and postcolonial "civil" wars flourished. Newly independent India and the then-impoverished post–World War and post–civil war China took formative roles in the creation of the Non-Aligned Movement of postcolonial states. Given this context in economically developing countries, one might expect that the post–Second World War appearance of the academic subfield of development economics would reflect on the connection between economy and war in the development process. But what had become true of the larger debate between Austrians and Marxians, now complemented by the addition of Keynes's macroeconomics, also proved true in development economics: an orthodoxy developed and came to rule the economics discipline. Thus Arthur Lewis, Gunnar Myrdal, Theodore Schultz, Hans Singer, Raul Prebisch, and Walt Rostow were among the early giants in the subfield. Of different intellectual persuasions, their debate resulted in the descendants of Austro-marginalists eventually prevailing academically and institutionally. Questions of development were separated from conflict, not to be joined again until the emergence of a narrowly conceived conflict economics, especially after the post–cold war era, since the early 1990s (see Section 4).

Meanwhile, in industrialized states, the Marxian underconsumptionist view of military expenditure in creating demand was linked to naïve Keynesian macroeconomics, in which military expenditure, as one component of government spending, engenders effective demand and subsequent multiplier effects.[13] Military spending can be helpful to an economy, even as it was generally accepted that war has a negative effect on economies. "Military Keynesianism," as it was dubbed, was given an *institutionalist* cloak, predicated

---

[13] The discussion in this paragraph is based on Toporowski (2017) and Cyper (2018).

on the existence of a military-industrial complex (MIC) where vested interests exercise political pressure to force increases in military spending independent of external threat. Famously, even US President Eisenhower – an ex-general – warned the nation in his 1961 farewell address about the MIC and its self-serving operation.[14] In this, he was joined by prominent economists, post-Keynesian John Kenneth Galbraith and Marxian Michal Kalecki among them, who saw that military Keynesianism could work in an economy below full employment but (like Eisenhower) harbored reservations because of a MIC. Among the worries they and others, like Seymour Melman's *The Permanent War Economy* (1974), expressed was a concern that militarism might reduce civil technological pursuits and leadership that formed the basis for economic growth in the modern world. An explicit Marxist perspective of the MIC is provided by Mary Kaldor (1982), who sees the arms production system as a cause of militarism and as driving arms races.[15]

In the inaugural issue of the *Cambridge Journal of Economics*, Ron Smith (1977) reviewed the underconsumptionist explanation of the role of military expenditure in capitalism. He argued that a more complex Marxist explanation was needed to better understand the manner in which military expenditure influenced capitalism. Pivetti (1992, 1994) made Keynesian-style effective demand arguments for the positive role of military spending in the United States, arguing that it was a deliberate instrument of economic policy, used by governments to deal with economic downturns and unemployment, and that military expenditure has a salutatory, stimulating effect on the economy. Smith and Dunne (1994) show that the evidence does not support this assertion. More recently, Elveren (2019) has suggested that military expenditure does indeed have a positive effect on the general profit rate, but this does not translate into positive effects on the rate of economic growth if the large empirical literature is to be believed (Dunne and Tian 2020).

A rich body of heterodox literature has made important strides in helping us understand the nature, role, and effect of military expenditure and militarism in capitalism, a literature that we summarily labeled *military economics* in Section 1 (see also Smith 2011). Capitalism has changed and so has the military sector. Nevertheless, much of the analysis summarized here still is relevant and valid when the data and methodologies are updated to today's standards. An active research field, this type of work often is also published in subject areas other than economics.

---

[14] The speech is available at www.youtube.com/watch?v=Gg-jvHynP9Y.

[15] Mary Kaldor is a daughter of renowned economist Nicholas Kaldor. Another daughter is Frances Stewart, whose work we will encounter in Section 8.

4 Neoclassical and Neo-Keynesian Views

If classical economists, marginalists, Marxians, and Keynes are the grandparents of modern economics, what about their descendants? This section moves from *war economics* and *military economics* (Sections 2 and 3) to recapitulate the intellectual history of the other subfields outlined in Section 1, *defense*, *security*, narrowly conceived *conflict*, and *peace economics*.

> It might not be entirely incorrect to say that the majority of today's conflict and peace literature is empirical. But its underlying conception and theoretical foundations largely are neoclassical and neo-Keynesian

Perhaps the majority of today's conflict and peace literature is empirical with the theoretical underpinnings largely of neoclassical and neo-Keynesian form – hence the section's title. Parentage is important, as many contemporary researchers and, by implication, policy makers seem scarcely aware of their inheritance, on the basis of which arguments, empirical investigations, and policies are developed. One reason for this is that economics in the post–Second World War era became utterly dominated by mathematical techniques. Of course, prominent antecedents exist, but massive advances came with the 1944 publication of John von Neumann's and Oskar Morgenstern's *Theory of Games and Economic Behavior* and, in 1947, Paul Samuelson's *Foundations of Economic Analysis*. Mathematical economics and statistics became graduate school norms of *how to learn to do* economics and what it meant *to be* an economist. The prior preponderance of narrative reasoning was pushed onto the sidelines and a new standard arose: if a narrative argument could not be mathematically harnessed, it would be left to fend for itself in the wilderness areas of academic publishing. This was not quite fair play, as renowned economists such as Nicholas Kaldor and Joan Robinson chose to eschew formalism for its own sake. Even Keynes, mathematically trained and author of *A Treatise on Probability* (1921), questioned the technical approach. Even within the newly emerged orthodoxy, though, the relations between and among conflict, war, peace, and economy needed to be understood and dealt with as practical matters of politics and policies. Done mathematically and statistically or otherwise, this section details some of the field's work and developments since the Second World War.

4.1 Defense Economics

If defense economics has a formal period of emergence, it might be the early 1960s with the publication of Charles Hitch's and Roland McKean's *The Economics Defense in the Nuclear Age* (1960) and the day (21 January 1961)

Robert McNamara took office as the US government's Secretary of Defense. Leaving as chief executive officer of the Ford Motor Corporation, McNamara brought with him a gaggle of "whiz kids," experts in fields such as game theory, operations research, and economics. Their job was to apply *economics* to the big defense questions of the day, including defense budgeting, arms procurement, armed forces staffing, (nuclear) arms rivalries, and how to think through the operation of military alliances. Defense was an economic output, the production of which required inputs of men, materiel, and institutions, and why not do that *efficiently*? Many of the experts came from the RAND Corporation in Santa Monica, California, an affiliation that continues to this day. Notable RAND economists included Kenneth Arrow, Robert Aumann, Alain Enthoven, Charles Hitch, Howard Margolis, Harry Markowitz, Roland McKean, John Nash, John von Neumann, Edmund Phelps, Paul Samuelson, Thomas Schelling, Lloyd Shapley, Herbert Simon, Oliver Williamson, and Richard Zeckhauser, a list that includes what would become many future economics Nobel Prize recipients. Intellectually, most resembled Grandma Austria, via her marginalist revolution Walrasian–Hayekian line, rather more than they resembled Grandpa Marx. Even those who descended via Keynes tended to evolve into orthodox-leaning neo-Keynesians, rather than into heterodox-oriented post-Keynesians.

> If defense economics has a policy date of birth, it might be 21 January 1961, the day Robert McNamara took office as the US government's Secretary of Defense. With him, he brought a slew of experts to apply distinctively *economic* reasoning to the big defense questions of the day. Heterodox voices have had relatively little influence on defense policy and practice.

Samuelson's "The Pure Theory of Public Expenditure" (1954) parceled out "ordinary private consumption goods" from "collective consumption goods," relabeled "public good" in a 1955 follow-up article. National defense became the quintessential example of a public good. Spelling out many implications, Olson's *The Logic of Collective Action* (1965) built on that distinction and was followed by Olson's and Zeckhauser's "An Economic Theory of Alliances" (1966). Although conceived as a general theory of "the working of international organizations," it nevertheless deliberately employed the example of the North Atlantic Treaty Organization (NATO), a defense alliance, to make the theory's point, the theoretical and empirical investigation of which continues to this day (although NATO is now seen as an example of a club good).

Eventually, there arose the idea of regional and global public goods – for example, in Kaul, Grunberg, and Stern's UNDP-sponsored *Global Public Goods* (1999) – and of corresponding regional and global public bads, foremost among them mass atrocities and wars, with ill effects that can affect millions of "consumers," i.e., victims of war, from which they cannot feasibly exclude themselves. Thus spatial reach became another property of publicness, to which was added the property of "aggregator technologies" – that is, how the nature of parties' contributions to the public good or bad determines its overall level of provision (Hirshleifer 1983). For example, a regional defense alliance, such as NATO, is not simply the result of the equally weighted sum of members' contributions but more likely depends on the heft of its greatest, best-shot, contribution, namely that of the United States (Cornes and Sandler 1984).

On the (nuclear) strategy front, the classic works are Schelling's *The Strategy of Conflict* (1960) and *Arms and Influence* (1966). This was preceded and followed by a wider literature on arms rivalries and arms races. In the posthumously published *Arms and Insecurity* (1960), the polyglot Lewis F. Richardson developed the first mathematical model of an arms race. Based on his work in numerical weather forecasting, he introduced differential equations to ask how changes in a country's military stockpile in response to a rival's stock of weapons might evolve over time. Would a system of two countries come to a stable equilibrium and, if so, at what level of armaments? Would an equilibrium even exist? His work led to a rise in the mathematical study of strategic interdependencies. Follow-up examples include Kenneth Boulding's (1962) and Michael Intriligator's (1975) extensions. Later work modeled dyads such as India and Pakistan and Greece and Turkey, especially in the form of military expenditure rather than of weapons. (Hartley 2020 provides an overview of defense economics).

Arms rivalries presume the existence of weapons, and McNamara's whiz kids began to explore the economics of arms procurement, including questions of contracting under monopsony and, increasingly, under bilateral monopoly (Peck and Scherer 1962). From procurement, it was but a short step to investigate the economics of the global arms trade. Offering the opportunity of volume production, the better to reduce unit costs for the home defense market, it will by now be clear that even in the absence of outright war, economics had an outsized role to play in understanding and shaping nation-states' defense sectors. Unsurprisingly, then, defense economists also investigated the economics of military labor markets, the most dramatic example of which concerned this question: Which is better – to conscript a nation's young people into its armed forces or else to hire them as volunteers off the civilian labor market in competition with the private sector? To coerce or to seduce, that was the question. We see here the connection to Austrian-marginalist thought especially clearly. Conscription is an in-kind tax to be borne by a random selection of young people, mostly men. Drafted by lottery, they must defer educational advancements or forego civilian labor market opportunities they otherwise would have had. This does not sit well with the notion of freedom of choice and voluntary exchange and befuddles common sense – which other tax is imposed by lottery? Conscription was not *efficient*. Even before it finally extricated itself from the Vietnam war in 1976, the United States switched recruitment policy, in 1973, to an all-volunteer force. The policy has been followed ever since with the majority of nation-states having adopted it as well.

Heterodox voices have had relatively little influence on defense policy. Certainly, those voices have issued valuable critique and insights, for example on matters of defense budgeting, on the relation of those budgets to the larger government budget, and to deficit financing, debt accumulation, and the national economy, to name a few. While academically well-respected, critical perspectives have been more likely to be heard among nongovernmental organizations than within the halls of industrial and governmental power.

4.2 Security Economics

Security economics is more broadly conceived than the "mere" defense of national boundaries from external aggression. Attacks by terror organizations are a case in point. Already there had been a well-established, if small, literature on the economics of transnational terror, but with the 9/11 attacks on various sites in the United States, the topic attracted wide attention among economists. Whereas the literature on *transnational* terror attacks might well be grouped within defense economics, it is not obvious that *domestic* terror fits the same rubric. Add in the private sector's increased interest in, and expenditure on, perimeter surveillance and intrusion barriers; cybersecurity; biometric or other access control to specific laboratories, equipment, or information; ubiquitous video-surveillance in shops, restaurants, and sporting venues; x-ray or other scanning of containers at sea- and airports; satellite-monitored transport by sea, air, and land; and so on. Security, one realized, was more than national defense.

Tilman Brück published "An Economic Analysis of Security Policies" (2005), which analyzed "the security economy from an economic perspective." At the time, this term – the *security economy* – was novel, and although the article restricted the analysis to this economy's *public policy* choices, it does point to the broader idea of viewing security as risk management, for example via insurance markets. Apart from businesses, another part of the private sector are households, which also routinely insure against risk and incur additional expenses, from home burglar alarms to carbon monoxide detectors and fire extinguishers. The security economy is vast, even vaster were one willing to bundle in the well-established field of the *economics of crime*, which goes back to Gary Becker's 1968 classic "Crimes and Punishment: An Economic Approach." Published in the esteemed *Journal of Political Economy*, it could hardly have been more neoclassical in conception and execution than it was.

And another realization dawned, namely that the defense of a nation-state need not coincide with the security of its citizens. Overbearing rulers' abuse of armed state forces against their own citizens and the growing worldwide unease of humanity being held hostage to a pair of nuclear weapons–tinged super-powers wrangling over geopolitical positioning led to the notion of *human security* as distinct from national security secured by defense forces. A seminal publication, under the guidance of Pakistani economist Mabhub ul Haq, was the United Nations Development Program's (UNDP) 1994 *Human Development Report*. Laying out seven dimensions of human security (economic, food, health, environment, personal, community, and political), it harked back to the freedom from fear and freedom from want aspects of Roosevelt's famous 1941 four freedoms speech. (The other two were freedom of speech and freedom of worship.)

In contrast to establishment defense economics, security economics – especially in its human security conception – included among its pioneers renowned development economists of heterodox learning and leaning.

Of some importance is that the United Nations Development Programme (UNDP), an intergovernmental development agency and think tank, included among its report's panel of consultants renowned development economists such as Meghnad Desai, Keith Griffin, Stephany Griffith-Jones, Amartya Sen, Hans Singer, and Paul Streeten, virtually all of whom had some heterodox learning and leaning. Also of importance is that the 1994 report appeared in the wake of the end of the cold war superpower rivalry. As their direct political and economic interest in much of the Third World diminished, the metaphorical top blew off the boiling cooking pot in Africa and elsewhere. Long-simmering conflicts broke out in open wars, no longer suppressed by a now-absent USSR and a now-largely-disinterested United States. As scant development successes were threatened and even reversed by intrastate war, quantitative political scientists and economists took note. Conflict economics (in its narrow sense) emerged.

4.3 Conflict Economics

The origin of the *conflict economics* term lies in its broad theoretical conception, wherein violence is an option, not a necessity. Pioneering works from the 1950–80s by Kenneth Boulding, Thomas Schelling, Walter Isard, and Jack Hirshleifer come to mind, each developing a followership. *Conflict and Defense, The Strategy of Conflict, The Dark Side of the Force: Economic Foundations of Conflict Theory, International and Regional Conflict: Analytical Approaches*, and *Understanding Conflict and the Science of Peace* are titles of some of the books they produced. This was before the field differentiated into subfields. Narrowly understood conflict economics emerged strongly in the 1990s as the number and severity of civil wars notably increased with the advent of the end of the cold war era and its immediate aftermath and academics sought to understand their causes, conduct, and consequences. With Oxford economist and Africanist Paul Collier's appointment as director of the Development Research Group of the World Bank from 1998 to 2003 on the one hand and the increasing availability of conflict and national statistics on the other, the late 1990s and early 2000s saw an explosion of often high-profile quantitative analysis of civil war, often employing neoclassical and neo-Keynesian micro- and macroeconomic reasoning.

This still rapidly developing literature began with a focus on understanding conflict vulnerability at a national level. Especially on the theoretical front, scholars sought to understand rebels' use of violence. The underlying methodology is mostly neoclassical, examples of which are discussed in Section 7. Meanwhile, the empirical literature began exploring political, sociological, and economic factors behind the vulnerability of nation-states. Examples of political factors include war vulnerability due to decolonization, lower levels of democracy, government use of violence, and states' (in)capacity to respond to rebellion. Among social features, research included demographic characteristics and measures of differences along ethnolinguistic and religious dimensions. Key economic factors used included per capita GDP, poverty, international trade, and unemployment. Anderton and Carter's textbook (2019, pp. 251–2) details the theoretical and empirical literatures.

Key early differences in the empirical literature can be grouped into two categories. One relates to the definition of civil war itself and the other to the interpretation of how economic factors matter for the likelihood of war. Defining civil (or intrastate) war as "violent conflict within a state between a government and one or more internal opposition groups, with sizeable combatant or battle-related fatalities" (Anderton and Carter 2019, p. 229) requires the further definition of "sizeable." Whereas Fearon and Laitin (2003) count cases with as few as one hundred battle-related deaths per year (and a total of at least one thousand deaths for the duration of the war), Collier and Hoeffler (2004) take a threshold of one thousand battle-related deaths per year. Different samples and different empirical findings result, of course, but these also are driven by different theoretical priors. Fearon and Latin focus on "conditions that favor insurgency," which include political instability, rough terrain, large populations, and generalized poverty. All these characterize weak states and facilitate rebel recruitment for guerilla warfare. In contrast, Collier and Hoeffler's famous "Greed and Grievance in Civil War" paper argues that while "rebellion may be explained by atypically severe grievances," it might better be explained by "atypical opportunities" for building and sustaining rebel organizations' viability. The two studies are, nevertheless, complementary in that both find support for nongrievance factors for civil war onset risk.

A different cluster of studies focused on war duration and geographic spread. Early studies explored statistical relationships with cross-national data. As more country-level and geocoded data sets became available, in particular the Uppsala Conflict Data Program/International Peace Research Institute, Oslo (UCDP/PRIO) data sets, studies pivoted to the in-country spread of war and to the importance of geography more generally. The development of increasingly powerful statistical techniques also permitted ever more detailed studies of the spillover of war across and within countries (e.g., Silwal 2013). A significant development has been the analysis of the microlevel cost of violent conflict, especially via the Households in Conflict Network coordinated by Tilman Brück in Germany, Patricia Justino in the United Kingdom, and Philip Verwimp in Belgium. Studies exploit spatial and temporal variation in war intensity to causally identify short-term and long-term economic and human development effects of internal strife (e.g., Silwal 2017). Scholarship now is expanding to include consideration of pre- and postwar cultural norms and the institutional legacies of violent conflict. Another stream of work has recognized that parties do not always have an interest in settling disputes. War can benefit certain individuals or groups, including external players such as arms-supplying nation-states and various middlemen, with little incentive to agree to peaceful conflict resolution.

A rich literature produced by a global cast of researchers and assembled in specialist research journals, *Handbooks*, and other collected volumes of essays and articles testifies to the coming-of-age of conflict and peace economics as a well-established and well-recognized field of study.

Apart from the bibliographic notes in Anderton and Carter's text (2019), the interested reader can also study amply referenced review articles by Blattman and Miguel (2010), Verwimp, Justino, and Brück (2019), Gaibulloev and Sandler (2019), and Anderton and Brauer (forthcoming). Also testifying to the burgeoning interest is the slew of specialized peer-reviewed research journals, including the *Journal of Conflict Resolution* (since 1956), the *Journal of*

Peace Research (1964), *Conflict Management and Peace Science* (1973), *Defence and Peace Economics* (1990), *Peace Economics, Peace Science and Public Policy* (1993), *The Economics of Peace and Security Journal* (2006), and the *International Journal of Development and Conflict* (2011), along with an impressive array of handbooks and other volumes of collected essays and articles.

4.4 Peace Economics

Despite the liberal appearance of the word "peace" in the aforementioned research journals, it is predominantly war that is the subject matter of study. A normative desire for peace drives those studies, but scholars focus on the conditions and circumstances giving rise to violence as if peace were its mere symmetric absence. While symmetry is not necessarily implied, comparative studies of why some communities experience war and others peace still are rare. Jha (2007) gets close in that he asks why some Hindu-Muslim communities in India have experienced a millennium of peaceful coexistence, whereas elsewhere on the subcontinent intercommunal violence has been common. He highlights certain institutional designs that created economic benefits for maintaining peace. This chiseling out of design features is picked up in Brauer and Dunne (2012) and Brauer and Caruso (2013), who define peace economics in regard to the design of institutions.

On the political front, institution-building first came in the form of regularizing and resetting international rules for commercial and monetary relations among the forty-four Second World War allied nations who created new norms of behavior as set out in the 1944 Bretton Woods Agreement and formation of the International Monetary Fund and the International Bank for Reconstruction and Development (now part of the World Bank Group). This was followed politically by the 1945 signing of the Charter of the United Nations by fifty founding members. There followed the rebuilding of western Europe. Of special importance was George C. Marshall's eponymous plan. The US Army Chief of Staff during the war, he became the US Secretary of State and in 1947 gave a short speech at Harvard University that laid out the specifically American reasons for aiding Europe, including the defeated Germany.[16] To quote:

> Aside from the demoralizing effect on the world at large and the possibilities
> of disturbances arising as a result of the desperation of the people concerned,
> *the consequences to the economy of the United States* should be apparent to
> all. It is logical that the United States should do whatever it is able to do to

---

[16] See www.marshallfoundation.org/marshall/the-marshall-plan/marshall-plan-speech/.

assist in the return of normal economic health in the world, without which there can be no political stability and no assured peace. [Emphasis added].

This harked back to Keynes's famous 1919 tract *The Economic Consequences of the Peace*, in which Keynes eviscerated the provisions of the Treaty of Versailles that, if implemented, surely would reduce Germany to penury and ignite its desire to rise again, vengefully, as indeed it did. And in pointing out that peace in Europe is crucial for economic prosperity in the US, Marshall appealed to America's enlightened self-interest. Shortly thereafter, in Europe, Jean Monnet prepared a plan for Robert Schuman, the French foreign minister, that in agreement with Germany's new chancellor Konrad Adenauer set in motion what would become today's largely peaceful European Union.

Where institutions can succeed to create and maintain peace, so also can they fail. Heterodox economists especially have critiqued postwar economic policies that often appear to recreate the very institutions, vested interests, and pressures that give rise to war in the first place. Partly as a consequence, conflict and peace economists increasingly tie into the larger field of mechanism design to study the economic incentives, disincentives, and tradeoffs involved in creating norms and in designing institutions (Swee 2016), a theme briefly taken up in Section 8.

Having provided a broad sweep of the history of thought of conflict and peace economics, the next three sections explore selected themes, theories, and evidence in more detail. Section 5, indeed, picks up on the theme of institutions, showing how *domestic* institutions even of victorious states can fall prey to militarism and adversely skew the domestic (political) economy. Section 6 examines the economics of military expenditure and the cost of war, and Section 7 delves into a selection of neoclassical theories and their extensions. All this is followed in the concluding Section 8 with what we believe are underexplored and altogether missing topics that the field will need to address in the future.

Part III   Selected Theory and Evidence
5 Conflict and the Growth of Government

This section discusses how preparing for and engaging in war can unfavorably change the fabric of *domestic* institutions. The issue is that while expansions in state power may be used to protect domestic liberties, they can also be used to undermine domestic freedom. This aspect of state-provided defense, often overlooked by economists, is important because the costs of defense and war often are greater than what is captured by explicit monetary outlays or observable defense-related activities.

5.1 Differentiating between Scale and Scope

How does preparing for, and engaging in, conflict affect domestic political institutions? Writing in 1795, one of the US "founding fathers," James Madison (1865, p. 491), provided his thoughts on this question:

> Of all the enemies to public liberty war is, perhaps, the most to be dreaded, because it comprises and develops the germ of every other. War is the parent of armies; from these proceed debts and taxes; and armies, and debts, and taxes are the known instruments for bringing the many under the domination of the few. In war, too, the discretionary power of the Executive is extended; its influence in dealing out offices, honors, and emoluments is multiplied; and all the means of seducing the minds, are added to those of subduing the force, of the people. . . . No nation could preserve its freedom in the midst of continual warfare.

Madison emphasized that war can influence growth in both the scale *and* scope of government. *Scale* refers to the size of government, typically measured through aggregate indicators such as expenditure on the military or by the number of people employed in military-related matters. The increase in expenditure, taxes, and debts that Madison referred to all are matters of scale. *Scope*, in contrast, refers to the range of activities undertaken by government. When Madison warned about increases in the discretionary power of government associated with war, he was highlighting the importance of scope.

Scale refers to the size of the government. *Scope*, in contrast, refers to the range of activities taken by government. For the most part, economists have neglected issues of scope.

To understand why scope matters, consider a scenario where a government allocates resources to military expenditure. These expenditures provide insight into the scale of government but not the scope of its activities, as they might be spent on defending the property and person of the domestic populace, or they might be used to repress and undermine the liberties of that same populace. The example illustrates that indicators of scale say nothing about how those resources are used. For the most part, economists have neglected issues of scope and instead focus mainly on the scale of government activities. This literature emphasizes, for example, the theoretical and empirical aspects of war and the scale of government (Peacock and Wiseman 1961; Hughes 1977, p. 209; Peltzman 1980, p. 214; Porter 1980; Rockoff 1999) and of military expenditure and economic growth during and after conflict (see Section 6).

The neglect of the scope aspect of government growth associated with war can be explained by three factors (Coyne 2015, p. 390; Coyne and Hall 2018, pp. 15–6). First, economists assume that scale and scope are correlated and move together (see for instance Peltzman 1980, p. 209). A possibility, this need not be the case as the state's fiscal scale may remain constant, or even decrease, yet its scope might increase. Consider government surveillance. Advances in technologies allow governments to monitor the activities of both domestic and foreign people more efficiently and at lower costs than ever before. Under this scenario, the scale of government – that is, the dollars spent on surveillance – might remain constant or shrink, even as the scope of government power over the lives of private persons expands.

Second, scope is harder to measure than scale. As Nobel Laureate James Buchanan (1975, p. 163) noted, in matters of public finance, "it is more difficult to measure the growth of Leviathan in these [scope] dimensions than in the quantifiable budgetary dimensions of the productive state." Scale can be captured in readily available aggregate figures making it easy to see the amount of resources being spent on different general government functions (for example, entitlements, defense, and education). An equivalent aggregate measure of the scope of government activities does not exist. Understanding the range of government activities requires a detailed analysis of context-specific circumstances to understand the nuances of government actions and how they have evolved over time.

Third, the model of state-provided defense employed by economists minimizes concerns related to the scope of government activities. For most economists, "defense" tends to be an all-encompassing category, assumed to be a public good provided in optimal qualities and quantities by a benevolent government. As Dunne (1995, p. 409) notes, the neoclassical approach to defense provision "is based on the notion of a state with a well-defined social welfare function, reflecting some form of social democratic consensus, recognizing some well-defined national interest, and threatened by some real or apparent potential enemy." Given these assumptions, there is no need to focus on the scope of government activities because the state is assumed to be doing exactly what is necessary to maximize social welfare. These assumptions are problematic, given that expansions in discretionary state power associated with preparing for, and engaging in, war have historically reduced domestic individual liberties (Linfield 1990, Porter 1994, Rehnquist 1998, Schlesinger, Jr. 2004, Irons 2005, Cole and Dempsey 2006, Cole and Lobel 2009, Walker 2012, Coyne and Hall 2018). The main takeaway from this scholarship is that the state's military activities are not neutral with respect to domestic institutions – economic, legal, political, and social. Instead, the state's activities can, and do, have real, long-lasting effects on the fabric of domestic life as state power expands at the expense of the power possessed by individuals. It is important, therefore, for economic treatments of conflict and the growth of government to incorporate these dynamics to understand how military-related activities can affect domestic institutions through changes in both the scale *and* scope of domestic government.

5.2 Economic Models of War and the Growth of Government

5.2.1 Scale of Government

The scholarship on war and the scale of government identifies several channels through which conflict might permanently increase expenditures during and after war (see Dunne 1996; Smith 2000; and Dunne, Smith, and Willenbockel 2005 for a detailed review).[17] Some scholars find that government expenditure does not permanently increase in the aftermath of war. For example, Tussing and Henning (1974) find no evidence of a postwar increase in US government expenditure for the 1900–69 period. Rockoff (1999) considers several dimensions – spending, increased agency employment, creation of new agencies, and creation of new regulations – of possible government growth in the United States following the Second World War and does not find evidence for war-related increases in any of these categories. Other scholars find quite the opposite. Peacock and Wiseman (1961) argue that a large portion of the increase in public expenditure in the United Kingdom during the 1890–1955 period can be attributed to wartime factors, such as the public's willingness to accept expanded government services and pay more taxes. Hughes (1977, p. 209) argues that expenditure in the postwar period increases because of new interest payments, veteran's benefits, and an overall increase in government costs that persist following conflict. Porter (1980) argues that war leads some federal agencies to increase their number of employees. In the postwar period, there are some cutbacks, but employment remains higher than in the prewar period, resulting in a permanently larger scale to finance the expanded state. Smith (2020) analyzes the relationship between debt and defense spending in the United Kingdom over a three-century period (1700–2016), finding "a robust relationship between the share of military expenditure and the change in national debt, reflecting debt financing of wars, even after controlling for nominal income growth and the long interest rate" (p. 421).

Although in the minority, some economists have studied how the *scope* of state power can increase due to the military activities of the state. The most notable is Higgs's (1987, 2012) analysis that appreciates and incorporates the

---

[17] A separate but related literature explores the distortionary effects of military expenditure on domestic economic activity (Melman 1970, 1974; Duncan and Coyne 2013; Coyne 2020, pp. 24–9).

interconnections among scale, scope, and power. To understand the specific mechanisms and conditions behind the growth of government, Higgs (1987) develops a comprehensive theory of the ratchet effect.[18] In his theory, the all-inclusive size – that is, scale *and* scope – of the state increases during times of crisis, including wars. Higgs's model includes five stages. The first is *normality*, which refers to the pre-crisis period. The second stage is *expansion*, which refers to the increase in the size (some combination of increases in the scale and scope) of government in response to crisis. In Higgs's framework, expansion is initially driven by citizens' ideology, which leads them to demand that government "do something" to address the crisis. Expansions can be either direct (for example, in state control over economic decision-making) or indirect (for example, in institutional precedents enabling future expansions in state power). Higgs emphasizes that many of the costs associated with these expansions in state power are not readily observable to ordinary citizens. It is difficult for citizens to gauge accurately the cost of things like regulations, economic controls, forced reallocations of resources, and inflationary finance associated with war efforts. This imperfect information on the part of citizens allows the government to implement policies without citizens realizing the full magnitude of the associated cost. The result is that the cost of the government's response to crisis is understated (Higgs 1987, pp. 62–7). The third stage is *maturity*, where the growth of post-crisis government has reached its peak. This is followed by the fourth stage, *retrenchment*, where the size of government begins to shrink relative to the peak. The final stage is *post-crisis normality*, which refers to the status quo in the wake of the crisis. Critically, the size of the post-crisis government, in the fifth stage, is larger than what would have existed absent the crisis.

Higgs outlines three reasons why a government's size, post-crisis, never returns to its pre-crisis size. First, new government agencies created during the crisis may continue to operate, even if on a smaller scale. Second, vested interests, which benefited from the largess associated with the crisis, have an incentive to perpetuate the status quo. Finally, and central to Higgs's theoretical framework, the activities of government during times of crisis can lead to changes in popular ideology, which offers continued support for bigger government – in scale and scope – well after the crisis ends (Higgs 1987, pp. 67–72). Crisis and the subsequent government response can affect the attitudes of several categories of key actors – private citizens, policy makers, and the judiciary – such that people become more accepting of a government that, relative to the counterfactual, is larger and more comprehensive in size. This change in attitude might, in turn, result from several factors.

---

[18] The term "ratchet" was first used by Porter (1980), discussing permanent expansions in the scale of the state due to war, but Higgs offers the most comprehensive theory of the ratchet effect.

First, people might lose confidence in the pre-crisis system and, as a result, become accepting of an expanded government role. Second, expansions in government during crisis often become normalized in daily life and no longer are viewed as extreme emergency activities. As a result, "many people are likely to learn to like, or at least to tolerate without active opposition, socioeconomic and political arrangements that appeared in the beginning to be unavoidable – but assuredly temporary – evils necessitated by a great social crisis" (Higgs 1987, p. 72). Together, these factors can contribute to the permanency of expansions in state power.

Overall, Higgs finds historical support for his theory of the ratchet effect across numerous crises throughout the history of the United States, including the two World Wars and the Great Depression. In a follow-up work, summarized in Higgs (2012), he applied this logic to contemporary events in the post-9/11 period associated with the US government's transnational war on terror.

5.2.2 Scope of Government

Coyne and Hall (2014, 2018) developed a "boomerang effect" theory to explain increases in the scope of government associated with foreign interventions. The logic is as follows. Preparing for and engaging in foreign intervention serves as a laboratory for the development and refinement of new forms of state-produced social control over foreign populations. These tools and techniques of social control are necessary for interveners, to ensure that they can achieve their desired outcomes in other societies. Under certain circumstances, such as when citizens grant government power to assuage their fears of threats or when domestic territory is part of the battlefield (for example, in the "war on drugs" and the "war on terror"), these innovations in social control are imported back to the intervening country. This expands the scope of domestic state activities over the lives of the populace.

The *boomerang effect* occurs when preparing for and engaging in foreign intervention serves as a laboratory for the development and refinement of new forms of state-produced social control. Under certain circumstances, these innovations are imported back to the intervening country. The effect sheds light on a range of historical and contemporary state activities usually left unquestioned and unexamined.

Three channels facilitate this importation. The *human capital channel* refers to the skills and knowledge related to social control developed by participants in foreign interventions, meaning the designers and implementers and those associated with these categories of actors. This unique human capital becomes part of the skill set of those involved in the design and implementation of the intervention. The *organizational dynamics channel* refers to the process through which those with this unique human capital change the structure and culture of domestic (public and private) organizations. Some of the participants in foreign interventions return to normal civilian life. Others enter the security complex, consisting of government agencies and private firms, and use their human capital in ways that shape and influence domestic life. This influence can involve taking on leadership roles in organizations or bringing techniques for effective social control initially developed for use abroad home. Finally, the *physical capital channel* refers to the development of tools that increase the efficiency of state-produced social control. Examples include surveillance and monitoring technologies, as well as weapons for efficiently controlling and killing potential and actual resisters and enemies. Together, these three channels contribute to an expansion of domestic social control by the state, resulting in changes in domestic institutions and the relationship between state and citizen. These expansions are not captured in traditional measures of scale. The number of people employed, for instance, does not capture the types of human capital they possess or their influence on the nature of government activities related to security.

The boomerang effect framework sheds light on a range of historical and contemporary state activities, including the US national surveillance state, the militarization of police in the United States, the domestic use of drones by the US government, and the domestic use of state torture in prisons in the United States (Coyne and Hall 2014, 2018). In each case, preparing for and engaging in foreign interventions led to an expansion in the scope of domestic state power. The general implication of this framework is that "the provision of what at first might appear to be productive state activities (e.g., national security and defense) may actually be predatory and unproductive by undermining domestic citizens' liberty and freedom. Even if the scale of government does not grow, foreign interventions can cause the scope of government activities at home to expand in an undesirable manner" (Coyne and Hall 2014, p. 20).

5.3 Conclusion

Scholarship on the growth of government emphasizes that domestic institutions cannot be assumed to be neutral with respect to the military activities of the state. The state's monopoly on military activities grants political decision makers significant power over citizens. This power can be used for good, but it also lowers the cost of the state controlling citizens and imposing harms.

Moreover, research on expansions in the scope of government indicates that the negative effects of the state's military activities are often long-lasting and variable, with the full cost being concealed by a focus on simple aggregates of scale, and that a neglect of the nuances for how military activities can change domestic institutions can result in potentially negative outcomes.

6 Military Expenditure, War, and the Cost of War

This section reviews the empirical literature on the impact of military expenditure on economic growth in developing countries and the impact of war itself. It also considers the empirical literature on the determinants and cost of intrastate war. This leads to a discussion of what these literatures tell us, namely that dealing with *postwar* economies requires different policy approaches than when dealing with nonwar developing economies.

6.1 Military Expenditure and the Economy

How military expenditure affects economic growth is a controversial question that continues to be debated among researchers, policy makers, and lobbyists. The relationship is inherently complex with the added difficulty that such spending, except in times of war, is really not that big a share of GDP, and its effect is likely contingent on country context, both historical and current. Factors such as the institutional structure of the country and what type of government is spending the funds can be important. Democracies tend to spend less on the military than autocracies, and the latter have less accountability and transparency in military budgeting and expenditure. Military spending has also been found to have larger negative economic effects on autocratic and transition states compared to democracies. Changes in internal or external threats that a country faces can also be important, as military expenditure may have a negative impact on economic growth, but in the face of external threats, it might be growth-enhancing. It may be less detrimental to growth when a country is a net arms exporter (Dunne and Tian 2013), and the impact may depend on how the money is spent (on salaries, equipment, or weapons imports) and on how that spending is financed. Methods of deficit financing are associated with different macroeconomic imbalances: money printing with inflation, foreign reserve use with the onset of currency crises, and foreign borrowing with external debt crises. Debt incurred to purchase arms can also influence domestic interest rates, with possible feedbacks to private and public sector investment levels (Dunne, Perlo-Freeman, and Soydan 2004), and it would also seem that being involved in the arms trade inevitably leads to being involved in, or close to, corruption (d'Agostino, Dunne, and Pieroni 2016).

How military expenditure affects economic growth is a controversial question that continues to be debated among researchers, policy makers, and lobbyists.

Understanding is further complicated by the lack of an agreed-upon theory. Indeed, much of economic theory does not have an explicit role for military expenditure as a distinctive economic activity. The empirical literature tends to focus on the direct link to economic growth. Possible indirect channels of influence, such as externality or spillovers, are seldom considered. Reasons for this include that each channel can potentially have both positive and negative effects on growth. Technology spinoffs and arms imports can introduce advanced product and process technology to local industry, although modern weapons systems are more likely to benefit from spin-ins from civil industry, and so the pursuit of military technology can displace resources for civilian production and negatively affect growth (Brzoska 1983; Brauer and Dunne 2012).

Much of the more recent empirical work has used some form of economic growth model and panel data methods. As longer time-series data have become available, dynamic specifications have been introduced into panel data methods. Studies differ in technical details, choice of functional form, stochastic specification, appropriate proxies, and so on. In addition, estimating the military expenditure to growth relation is difficult because the two-way causality between output and military expenditure can produce either positive or negative correlations (Dunne and Smith 2020). Another issue is that the numerous sources of military expenditure data use different definitions (Brauer 2019).

Recently, Dunne and Tian (2020) surveyed 231 studies. Table 1 shows that of 138 cross-country studies, only 20 percent found a positive effect of military expenditure on growth, while 44 percent found a negative effect. The remaining 36 percent had unclear results. For country case studies, the most common finding still is that of unclear results (46 percent), while positive and negative were found in 26 and 28 percent of the studies, respectively. Before 2000, cross-country studies were more likely to find unclear results, but when including post–cold war data and employing improved econometric techniques, newer studies predominantly show a negative relationship. Strikingly, throughout the pre/post–cold war time periods considered, there has been little support for asserting that military expenditure enhances growth, but it is also quite clear that historical context is important: country case studies can find a positive effect. Further research will need to disentangle this seemingly counterintuitive outcome.

Table 1 Military spending and growth relationship (Adapted from Dunne and Tian 2020, p. 13)

Type	No. Studies	% positive	% negative	% unclear
Cross-country	138	19.6	44.2	36.2
Case studies	93	25.8	28.0	46.2
Total	231	21.6	37.5	40.5
Post–cold war data				
Cross-country	77	19.5	49.4	31.2
Case studies	51	29.4	23.5	47.1
Total	128	22.7	39.1	38.3

6.2 Determinants of Violent Conflict

In the past, economists saw conflict and war as important economic concerns, but the analysis of *inter*state conflict in the post-Second World War period has mainly been the domain of international relations (Brauer, Dunne, and Tian 2019). *Intra*state war has been commonplace, increasingly persistent, and ever so violent; however, development economics textbooks only mention it in passing. Yet it is clear that one cannot have development without peace. The involvement of economists was increased when the World Bank set up its Conflict and Development project and moved the focus to the material basis of war. This certainly led to an increase in research but still had little impact on textbooks and teaching of conflict and peace economics, especially within development economics.

A range of theoretical perspectives inform intra- or civil war analysis, reflecting the interdisciplinary nature of the research and the relatively late involvement of economists. Political scientists focused on grievance determinants of war, with theories emphasizing how modernization could lead to disruption of social order, with social and economic change causing the breakdown of social cohesion and alteration of perceptions. These concentrated on the role of political repression, failing institutions, political transitions, and informational problems, which together with a failure to redress economic or political grievances can lead to conflict. An alternative was provided by constructivist theories, which emphasized the social construction of identity, rather than accepting it as some fixed attribute (see Section 8). It is then political mobilization that leads to civil war violence, with leaders constructing ethnic and social identity in ways that benefit themselves (Sambanis 2002).

Economists tended to consider greed- or opportunity-based determinants of conflict. Grossman (1991) modeled rebellion as an industry, and Hirshleifer

(2001) suggested rational agents could potentially misperceive opportunities and grievances because of asymmetric information and thus start a war. These theories suggest that the onset of civil war is linked to the ability of insurgents to make a profit or believe that they will – that is, the greed hypothesis (Coulomb and Dunne 2008). Of course, one could argue that the two are difficult to distinguish. An insurgent group with valid grievances soon will find they spend a lot of their time trying to get money in various ways to support their armed struggle. What looks like greed may well have started as grievance.

The contributions of Fearon and Laitin (2003) and Collier and Hoeffler (2004) have been outlined in Section 4 and are not repeated here. These two papers had a major impact on research and led to a large follow-up literature that has advanced our understanding (Blattman and Miguel 2010). The literature continued to develop and improve in a number of areas. First, political scientists questioned the apparent lack of statistical significance of variables that are proxies for objective grievance. This led to efforts to improve measurement and obtain better proxies. Natural resource–related data sets were improved; grievances were measured better, including of horizontal and vertical inequality; and better measures of weak institutions have become available as well. Second, attempts have been made to improve causal identification, but the identification problem remains (i.e., Does war cause poor economic outcomes or vice versa?), mostly due to difficulties in finding appropriate instruments to disentangle the direction of causality. Third, research into the possible spillover effects of war, creating war in other countries, have appeared in the literature and, with it, more attention has been paid to the plight and role of internal and external refugees. Fourth, questions have been raised about measures of violence and war. In the past, war tended to be defined as an event with a thousand or more battle-related deaths, and peace was defined as less than this. Initially developed for the study of "traditional" interstate war, this metric was continued to be used even after the focus shifted to intrastate war in the post–cold war era. Then seen as unsuitable, a definition of war with twenty-five or more battle-related deaths was applied more often. Fifth, concern with estimation methods, in particular not allowing for the fact that some countries are peaceful while others cycle in and out of war, and that a peace observation in a year for, say, Sweden, does not carry the same meaning as one for the Democratic Republic of the Congo, needed redress. Using a procedure to deal with this for the original greed–grievance models led to the grievance terms becoming statistically significant (Dunne and Tian 2019), for example.

Researchers have also begun to examine potential determinants, such as the set of extant institutions and colonial legacies. In quantitative studies of war prevalence in Sub-Saharan Africa, the imposition of artificial state borders, living in "bad neighborhoods," and warmer temperatures (increasingly so, in the face of climate change) have come to take center stage as explanatory variables of interest. There is also some debate over the effects of migration on war and vice versa (Brzoska and Fröhlich 2016; Dunne and Tian 2019).

6.3 The Cost of War

One reason for studying the causes of war is because war is so costly. To gain some idea of how costly it is, a relatively large body of literature has been developed (reviewed in Smith 2014). Collier (1999) estimated that civil war leads, relative to its counterfactual, to a reduction of around 2.2 percent of GDP *per war year*, a large reduction given how long such wars often last and thus pretty much wiping out any prior economic development. Updated estimates concur, with some researchers considering the cost to be overstated (Human Security Report) and others understated (Global Peace Index). In 2008, the UNDP's Bureau for Crisis Prevention and Recovery suggested that the economic cost of civil war lay somewhere between 1.7 and 3.3 percent of GDP per country per war year *before 1990*, but that the average reduction was about 12.3 percent of GDP thereafter. This loss of output is staggering, and while countries do recover, they do not do so for a good number of years. The World Bank's *World Development Report 2011* remarks that not a single fragile state afflicted by violence had achieved even one of the eight Millennium Development Goals then in effect (p. xi).

Legacy effects of war, such as on health outcomes, can be pronounced and long-lasting, and research points to even longer adverse effects for genocides (Dunne and Tian 2015; Anderton and Brauer forthcoming). War leads to many hidden casualties, and the devastation can mean people die years after the war ends, a legacy cost that is often ignored. Hunger and disease in postwar regions can prove more fatal than direct violence (Dunne 2013). Additionally, war creates an environment in which other forms of violence can be facilitated and which can remain when the war is supposedly over (Brauer and Dunne 2012 and Section 8).

Two main approaches are used to measure the economic cost of war. An economic growth approach reasons that if war affects economic performance, it should be through factors of production or technology, plus the institutions and culture that augments them. A trend comparison is made of the actual and likely growth paths with and without war, respectively (Brauer and Dunne 2012). One can also compare war economies to otherwise similar but peaceful ones. There is a potential problem in making comparisons, as countries at war could be fundamentally different from peaceful countries (compare, say, Botswana to Mozambique or Zimbabwe), so that bad postwar performance may reflect prewar conditions rather than damage by war (Dunne 2013). These models also do not include the destruction of household assets, the flight of capital, or the effect of uncertainty on the cost of capital, all of which can play important roles in economic recovery. Substantial killing in war affects the size and quality of the postwar labor force. Even if fatalities may be relatively few as a proportion of a population, related injuries and deaths due to destroyed health clinics, for instance, can significantly increase the adverse effects (Ghobarah, Huth, and Russett 2003). Institutions and economic networks also suffer damage, and this too can hamper growth, although there is little research on how they evolve, adapt, and decline in war. What effects a war has can also vary on just how a war started and why and how it ends, such as in stalemate or victory for one side (Blattman and Miguel 2010).

Another approach is the accounting method. In it, one tries to work out a fairly comprehensive schema that sets out direct and indirect costs and then finds values for as many of the headers as possible. A difficult task, it can only be attempted for case studies, and in most cases, there will be many missing values and "guesstimates." Another problem is that high costs might simply reflect high research effort rather than any real difference in war cost (Bozzoli, Brück, and Sottsas 2010).

6.4 Postwar Recovery and Reconstruction

Turning to postwar aspects, four phases of recovery and reconstruction indicate the different types of policies and interventions that will be required at different times (Harris 1999). First is the formal end of fighting and attempts to put any peace agreement into practice. Second is a period of rehabilitation and restoration. This will include the removal of limitations on civil activity, reestablishing civil law and institutions, disarming ex-combatants, demining roads, repatriating footloose financial capital, and the return of displaced persons. This stage provides an environment in which the civil economy can start to take over from the war economy. Third is a period of reconstruction or replacement: gaining financial resources for reconstruction, repairing or replacing physical capital and infrastructure, demobilization of combatants and resettlement, rehabilitating victims, (re) introducing democratic governance, developing and restructuring civil institutions, and beginning reconciliation. And fourth is a period of development and transformation: adopting and implementing a new societal vision, undertaking needed structural changes, establishing new institutions, and continuing reconciliation. This period is only likely to be successful if the other stages have been successful (Dunne 2017).

Developing postwar reconstruction policies is not a straightforward affair.

Developing policies for postwar reconstruction is not straightforward. Interventions that are careful to balance the demand for economic growth with demands for justice and human welfare are necessary. However, with economists broadly failing to understand the transition from war to peace, the default option often has been to introduce generic free-market policies via the World Bank and the International Monetary Fund. In exchange for receiving assistance, it has become virtually obligatory for postwar countries to undertake some form of short-term economic stabilization program to correct balance of payment problems and reduce the demand for imported goods while stimulating exports. Toward this end, programs typically involve currency devaluation, higher taxes and interest rates, and the reduction or removal of government services. Additionally, medium-term adjustment and economic reform programs are demanded that, to further reduce government budget deficits, include cuts in government staff and spending, freezes on wages and salaries, and privatization of government services. Much of this can clash with the sequencing of the recovery stages and limit postwar "peace dividend" harvests (Brauer and Dunne 2012).

One example is that of Mozambique, which had had a thriving cashew nuts processing sector. Fulfilling conditions of foreign assistance adversely affected the foreign exchange rate, and the sector ceased to be competitive internationally. In addition, restrictions on government spending led to unemployment, disorganized demobilization, generalized insecurity, and in time to a restart of the war. Premature cuts in government spending can prevent needed social reforms and projects that aim to lower tensions to achieve the very political stability needed to preserve peace (Dunne 2006). Another concern regards the effect war can have on rural household behavior and how this might affect responses to attempts at reconstruction. Providing agricultural infrastructure in postwar Mozambique, for example, did not lead to the expected food surpluses for urban areas because farm households did not feel secure enough to move beyond the subsistence production to which they had grown accustomed (Brück 2001).

6.5 Conclusion

Not all researchers see war as necessarily negative (Cramer 2006). After all, most modern nation-states owe their current form to violent upheaval and conflict, and war can have positive economic effects in removing bad leaders or leading to the introduction of structures and governance needed for generalized betterment.

While all this work has been valuable, numerous concerns persist. One is that the nature of war is changing (Section 8), and this carries important policy implications. The distinction between civil war protagonists and transnational terror groups is becoming less clear, such as Boko Haram in Nigeria. Another is that clear links to organized crime exist through illicit narcotics and smuggling, and again sometimes the distinction from war is blurred. This, too, complicates the theoretical and empirical study of war.

7 Neoclassical Theory: Extensions and Evidence

This section summarizes selected neoclassical-based economic theories and evidence that together help reveal important aspects of conflict and peace. It begins with a summary of the standard rational choice model and extensions to theoretical models and evidence from game theory. Then it considers social network models, which have advanced theory and evidence in terrorism and organized crime literatures, with scattered developments in war, mass atrocity, and conflict resolution literatures. This triad of models has been extended to formally account for psychological and sociocultural phenomena in conflict and peace contexts. Summarizing research along these lines, the section also points to research opportunities.

People weigh benefits against costs when choosing one from among several possible actions to take. This is the central premise of *neoclassical economics* (see Section 2). Benefits arise when an action promotes a person's objectives. Costs ensue because actions come at a price such as money, effort, or time spent (for example, on gathering pertinent information). These resources are limited and hence form binding constraints. When making decisions, people do their best given their constraints – they optimize – and in this narrow sense they are said to be rational decision makers. When constraints further include the actions of others, interdependencies arise but people still weigh benefits against costs, only more complexly so. Hence, game theory (the study of strategic interactions) is part of the neoclassical paradigm, as is a good portion of the literature on network economics which studies large numbers of interacting players. The *rational choice (or constrained optimization) model, game theory*, and *network models* all can include psychological and sociocultural factors – the domains of *behavioral and social economics* – yet still posit actors who seek to advance their goals given their constraints.

7.1 Constrained Optimization

A violence-producing organization's objective is to maximize utility (its benefits) from attacks against civilian and/or political targets. Think of a terror organization's

(TO) wish to attack shopping malls or embassies. It will have a limited budget from which to defray expenses that come in the form of an average cost or price per attack, one for civilian targets and another for political targets. Likewise, the average price of, say, bombings differs from that of hijackings or kidnappings. The higher the (total) cost, the more rapidly the budget is depleted. Prices and budgets are constraints. In the model, the TO will choose, subject to its constraints, whichever combination of political and civilian attacks, and by whichever method of attack, is expected to maximize its utility. This will be its *rational choice*. Again, *rational* refers not to the objective of doing harm but to the way the TO goes about its decision-making – it does its "best" given its constraints.

This implies three classes of policy interventions. First, budget or *income policies* seek to reduce a TO's resources, such as asset freezes or reducing money laundering options. So long as attack prices and the TO's preferences remain unchanged, reduced resources tighten the constraints, and should lead to fewer political *and* civilian attacks. This is a statistically testable proposition. Second, *preference policies* focus on changing a TO's preferences such that attacks are not utility enhancing, or less so than before. This may be done for instance by creating (more) opportunities to express dissent nonviolently, such as participation in political argument, settled via elections. Third are *price policies*. These seek to raise the relative price of attack. One option is to try to raise the cost of recruitment (hiring terrorists, the attacking labor force, being part of the price of attack). This approach lay behind the "winning hearts and minds" strategies the United States employed in Afghanistan and Iraq, attempts to turn enemies if not into friends then at least into neutrals. Another option is to harden political targets such as fortifying embassies and better protecting their personnel as some governments did following attacks against US embassies in Kenya and Tanzania in 1998. However, raising the cost of attacking political targets invites, according to standard theory's *substitution principle*, more attacks on civilian targets. While it is possible that a higher price of political attacks drains a TO's budget so much that both political and civilian attacks are reduced, it is also possible – depending on the TO's preferences – that the organization will cut back political attacks and substitute into a *greater* number of civilian attacks. Indeed, Enders and Sandler (2000, p. 330) warned of this very possibility prior to al Qaeda's 11 September 2001 attacks. In a word, the model can suggest unintended *but predictable* consequences of a policy of political target hardening (Gaibulloev and Sandler 2019).

The substitution principle is general and far-reaching in conflict and peace economics.

The substitution principle is general and far-reaching in conflict and peace economics. Rebel groups may substitute from landmines to child soldiers if landmines become more expensive (Anderton and Carter 2019, pp. 72–4), genocide perpetrators substitute attacks from one village to another if the former becomes better protected (Anderton and Brauer 2016, pp. 163–4), terror organizations substitute into kidnappings if airlines are better protected (Enders and Sandler 2012, p. 143), and restraining one type of weapon in an arms control agreement can enhance rivalry along another weapons class (Craft 2000). The list can be multiplied and, even then, is an account only of the substitution principle, let alone of other principles that standard theory entails.

7.2 Game Theory

In a game of chess, each player's move depends on the other player's moves. One, therefore, anticipates the other's possible moves to deduce what one's own current best move should be. This intertwining is known as *strategic interdependence*, which arises in many interactions, including in conflict and peace contexts. We illustrate this with the famous Prisoner's Dilemma game and, more broadly, in the context of the bargaining theory of war and peace.

7.2.1 Prisoner's Dilemma

The Prisoner's Dilemma (PD) game takes its name from a dilemma faced by each of two hypothetical prisoners. Captured and placed in separate cells, they are charged with a major crime which, upon conviction, carries a lifelong jail sentence. If there is lack of compelling evidence, and if the prisoners do not turn witness against each other, they each face only brief jail time on a minor charge. If in exchange for a less-than-lifelong sentence they each confess to the serious charge, each receives a lengthy, but not lifelong, sentence. But if one player confesses and turns witness against the other, who does not confess, then the first is offered freedom while the other receives the lifelong sentence. Even given the opportunity to communicate and coordinate their response, the *dilemma* is that each prisoner's best option is to confess and turn against the other, regardless of what the other chooses, and if both prisoners choose this option, they both receive the lengthy sentence. When a strategy is "best" in this way, it is called a *dominant strategy*. In PD, this result is remarkable as the joint, *socially* optimal outcome if neither confesses (minimal jail time for each) does not occur, since each player selects the *individually* best (dominant) strategy.

Generalized in two simple steps, the PD game finds wide application in conflict and peace economics. The first step is to rebrand the *not confess* strategy as the cooperative strategy (not confessing implies cooperation with the counterpart). The second step is to recognize that players can be all sorts of actors (for example, nations, NGOs, nonstate groups, individuals). What emerges is a *general model* for analyzing many conflict and peace dilemmas in which each actor follows its own self-interest and a suboptimal social outcome emerges. Consider, for instance, an arms rivalry between nations A and B as a PD game. The noncooperative strategy would be to build weapons at a rapid rate to try to get the upper hand, or at least not fall behind the rival. The result is a poor social outcome of relatively equal military power at the cost of foregone civilian goods production. Each nation would be better off if each restrained its accumulation of weapons. In attempting to achieve this better outcome, each, however, has an incentive to cheat. If they agree to restrain their weapons accumulation, what is to prevent either one (or both) from secretly building up its weapons stock anyway, thereby seizing the upper hand in the rivalry? Arms control is a recognition of the superiority of the cooperative outcome over the dominant strategy equilibrium in an arms rivalry. Given the incentive to cheat, most arms control agreements thus include verification protocols.

> The prisoner's dilemma setup has been applied to numerous conflict and peace contexts, including free riding among allies supporting peacekeeping missions, jointly conducted counterterror efforts, suboptimal provision of alliance defense, and incentives for both a government *and* a rebel group to attack civilians in war.

The PD setup has been applied in other conflict and peace contexts, including free riding among allies supporting peacekeeping missions (Sheehan 2011), jointly conducted counterterror efforts (Sandler and Siqueira 2009), suboptimal provision of alliance defense (Beyer 2018), and incentives for both a government and a rebel group to attack civilians in an intrastate war (Anderton and Carter 2019, pp. 299–301). The setup has also been extended to cover games with more than two players and how the PD's suboptimal outcome might be overcome with so-called trigger strategies that punish non-cooperation and/or reward cooperation or other institutional designs (Dixit, Skeath, and Reiley 2014).

7.2.2 The Bargaining Theory of War and Peace

The PD game involves implicit or explicit bargaining. In the arms rivalry game, the bargain is over an arms control treaty to achieve the cooperative outcome. Going to war is costly: people are injured or killed, assets destroyed, and economies disrupted. The question is: If war is costly, how can the bargain of peace (no war losses) possibly be missed? This seems to be a perplexing puzzle, and the bargaining theory of war and peace offers rationalist reasons to explain it.

One reason relates to issues of information, communication, and trust. Information may be incomplete through purposeful concealment or manipulation. Communication signals may be misrepresented, misunderstood, or may not reach decision makers in time, which can lead a player to rationally choose war (Fearon 1995). Other reasons include preemptive strikes on account of first-mover advantages, expected power shifts that can raise incentives for preventive war, indivisibilities (a desired object seemingly cannot be shared), and politically biased (toward war) leaders (Anderton and Carter 2019, pp. 184–94). The model also can be extended to account for psychological factors such as reference dependence and loss aversion and sociocultural phenomena such as malevolence (enjoying another player's decline even at one's own expense; Anderton and Carter 2019, pp. 194–8). In such extensions, peace is more difficult to achieve than the standard theory suggests.

Bargaining theory has also guided empirical inquiry. For example, Bas and Schub (2016) find that secret alliances, by fostering incomplete information, make conflict between states *more* likely. Adams (2003/4) considers how offensive-dominant military technologies *elevate* the risk of major power war. The roles of power shifts and *raised* incentives for preventive war receive empirical support in Bell and Johnson (2015). And while many forms of third-party intervention to promote peace have been found helpful, Narang (2015) finds, counterintuitively, that "humanitarian assistance can inadvertently *prolong* fighting by slowing down the accrual of information, [which] . . . prevents opponents from coordinating expectations about what each is prepared to accept in a settlement" (p. 185; our emphasis).

7.3 Network Economics

Human beings are quintessential "social critters." In conflict and peace economics, violence-producing and peace-promoting organizations likewise use networks to advance their respective goals. We illustrate the power of network thinking with Granovetter's (1978) thought experiment. Imagine one hundred individuals, each with a certain preference to participate in a riot against an oppressive government. Person 1 (the zealot) riots no matter what, even if none of the other ninety-nine does. Person 2 participates if at least one other person goes first. Person 3 riots if at least two others do, and so on to person one hundred, who riots if at least ninety-nine others riot. Consequently, all one hundred people will participate. But if person 2 catches a cold and does not show up, then person 3 will not be "activated" to participate in the riot and neither will persons 4 to 100. This is a stunning, complete reversal of the initial outcome! A seemingly trivial change (person 2 catches a cold) dramatically affects whether or not a riot emerges. Network theory finds that one can neither add up (aggregate) the preferences of individuals at the microlevel to infer a macro-outcome nor can one infer from the occurrence of a macro-outcome what the preferences of its participants were. Instead, it is the layer of interactions among networked actors – the *meso-level* – that connects micro-behaviors to macro-outcomes (Schelling 1978). That is profoundly important for understanding whether large-scale outcomes emerge or not. Moreover, network theory finds that this property of situational *emergence* of an outcome generally results in multiple possible equilibria on which a social system may settle, and each of which can be highly dependent on idiosyncratic conditions.

> Instead of either the micro- or the macro-level, it is the meso-level – the layer of interactions among networked actors that connects micro-behaviors to macro-outcomes – that is profoundly important for understanding whether large-scale outcomes emerge or not.

The relevance of networks is demonstrated in many empirical applications. Examples include the propagation of civil violence across multiple networked actors in the Democratic Republic of the Congo (König, et al. 2017), how trade networks can diminish war (Kinne 2012), and the causes and consequences of alliance networks (Maoz 2011). Network analysis has also been applied to study terror groups (Dziubiński, Goyal, and Vigier 2016; Enders and Jindapon 2010) and social connections that fostered participation during the 1994 Rwandan genocide (McDoom 2013). Other studies have used network explanations of why some Jewish victims during the Holocaust chose evasion and others uprising (Finkel 2017), along with why some religious groups rescued Jews and others did not (Braun 2019), and the elevated effectiveness of peace promotion that occurred when international NGOs were networked (Wilson, Davis, and Murdie 2016).

7.4 Extensions to Psychological and Sociological Factors

Actor choices often deviate from the predictions of the standard neoclassical model. For example, laboratory and field experiments suggest that people not only care about the *absolute* amount of some item (say, money or a consumer good) but also about the amount *relative* to some benchmark, a psychological feature the standard model ignores. Other experiments find that people are *loss averse*: a suffered loss weighs more, and sometimes far more, heavily on perceived well-being compared with an equivalent gain. Loss aversion behavior also is ignored in the standard model. Moreover, while the standard model assumes that individuals' preferences are fixed (*context independent*), sociologically informed economics finds instead that preferences are *context dependent*. For example, one's beliefs about with whom, or what, one identifies with and how one will act in the future may be overridden by a situational context such as that provided by peer influences when the future arrives. In the context of genocide, for instance, some "ordinary people" who participated as perpetrators later appear to show genuine befuddlement at and remorse for what they did (Waller 2007). This pre/post change can be explained in that the perpetrator's peer context of decision-making changed.

The good news is that many nonstandard elements are being integrated into the standard model, thus generating a richer, more general theory to understand human behavior, including conflict and peace behavior.

7.5 Conclusion

On neoclassical-inspired modeling, much more can be said than is covered here. Recommended follow-up readings include Anderton and Carter's (2019) textbook on conflict economics, Enders and Sandler's (2012) book and Gaibulloev and Sandler's (2019) survey on the economics of terrorism, and Anderton and Brauer's (forthcoming) survey on the economics of mass atrocities and their prevention. The neoclassical approach, with its long pedigree in the history of economic thought, has provided the workhorse models in conflict and peace economics. This does not mean that it is without weaknesses, even with the extensions we mentioned. In responding to criticism, however, neoclassical theory has developed ever more general models of human decision-making in which rational (standard benefits and costs), nonrational (psychological and sociocultural, but still fairly personal phenomena), and network-systemic (more impersonal, situational) aspects of decision-making and subsequent behavior are considered. This bodes well to further improve our understanding of, and policy responses to, conflict and peace challenges.

Part IV Conflict and Peace Economics: Where to Next?
8 The Future of Conflict and Peace Economics

Listed in this section are themes we believe are underexplored or altogether missing in the literature and in grave need of further research. The list is illustrative, not comprehensive. For brevity, some themes are mentioned only in passing; others are sketched out.

8.1 General Themes

First among the general themes is bioeconomic peace research. Humans not only will need to make peace with each other but with their planet, more so as mutual feedback effects from planetary destruction to interhuman conflict become more apparent, from climate change to the rapid spread of zoonotic diseases (Brauer and McDougal 2020). A *second* topic is that of weaponry. Defense economists have tended to focus on major conventional weapons (surface and submarine vessels, aircraft, and the like), yet have expended scarcely any effort to explore the economics of small arms, particularly of handheld firearms, which are today's primary weapons used in repression and war, and of the economics of "futuristic" arms such as dual-use neuro- and directed-energy weapons and the tools of cyberwar, neither of which are futuristic at all but already deployed and in use. *Third*, economists will need to reconsider the very notion of defense. Abraham Lincoln's reminder in 1863, given at Gettysburg in the midst of America's civil war, that the United States was "conceived in Liberty, and dedicated to the proposition that all men are created equal" and that scores of its soldiers had been sacrificed so "that government of the people, by the people, for the people, shall not perish from the earth" captures an ideal of *liberal democracy* under threat of reversal today when "defense" is turned inward toward undue surveillance and repression as often as it appears turned outward.[19]

> The trade in illicitly obtained cultural heritage objects, including items looted in war, is among the highest-grossing international crimes.

Fourth, many conflict-afflicted countries are rich in cultural heritage objects.[20] These are subject to looting or outright destruction in war. Resale of war loot on illicit art markets is among the highest grossing of international crimes (Bazley 2010), often funding violent organized crime, terror, or rebel groups. The losses deprive local communities of cultural practices and identity and, as markers of our common human heritage, also rebound to all current and future generations worldwide. They deserve economists' attention (Silwal 2021). *Fifth* are the macrofinancial aspects of migration, war-induced or not. Amounting to more than half a trillion US dollars in 2019,[21] many of the top remittances-receiving countries, as a percentage of GDP, are postwar or

---

[19] The text of Lincoln's delivered speech is disputed, as five differing versions of the text are in existence.

[20] A list of world heritage sites that are in danger is available at http://whc.unesco.org/en/danger/.

[21] www.worldbank.org/en/news/press-release/2020/04/22/world-bank-predicts-sharpest-decline-of-remittances-in-recent-history.

otherwise fragile states.[22] And *sixth* is the matter of culture, norms, and narratives that are relevant for conflict and peace economics. While norms have received considerable attention in the general economics literature (see, for example, Nunn and Wantchekon 2011, Moscona, Nunn, and Robinson 2020), narration is largely absent from the discipline (McCloskey 1983, Akerlof 2020). Stories people tell as events unfold become part of their motivation to act and shape individual behavior (Shiller 2017). Yet stories, as captured in ethnographic studies, for instance, have found little acknowledgment in conflict and peace economics, even as they may contain vital clues to understanding violence onset and, possibly, violence prevention. Scant research aside, such as those incorporating narratives in post-disaster recovery (Chamlee-Wright and Storr 2011), insights drawn from anthropological contributions have yet to be foregrounded.

8.2 Specific Themes

8.2.1 Inequality and Violence

The study of income inequality is as central to economics as is the study of production and exchange. Initially viewed through the lens of differential rates of return to the owners of production inputs – capital, land, and labor (that is, profits, rents, and wages) – economists delved into details such as those related to conceptual and measurement issues (Galbraith 2016; Trapeznikova 2019). In time, attention shifted from *income*-based measures (Lorenz curve, Gini coefficient, and Theil index) to outcome measures such as *well-being*. Anne Case and Angus Deaton's work pioneered the study of household consumption and poverty and helped institute detailed household data collections worldwide (Case and Deaton 1987). Sen and Foster (1997) incorporated normative concerns. Whereas these efforts focused on developing economies, Thomas Piketty (2015) has highlighted wealth concentration within industrialized countries.

> The study of inequality is as central to economic analysis as is the study of production and exchange.

Economic literature exploring the link between violent conflict and inequality is quite large. Early studies focused on the role of vertical inequality (among *individuals*); later studies added horizontal inequality (across *groups*). Pioneered by Frances Stewart (2016), the latter concept applies not only to

---

economic matters but also to inequality in opportunities for political participation (including in the armed forces, often a preserve for social elites), social aspects (access to human development services), and cultural status (recognition of a group's cultural practices). Each can play different roles in different places and may interact in different ways to give rise to a multiplicity of grievances that may result in the outbreak of violence. Measurement issues continue to arise, however. Sarntisart (2020), for example, shows that the required decomposition of gross inequality measures such as the Gini coefficient into *groups* of people is no straightforward matter and can give rise to substantial differences in statistical findings.

Little explored are the root causes of inequality among religious, cultural, and ethnolinguistic groups. Examining Hindu-Muslim violence in India, Mitra and Ray (2014) find that the relative increase in (majority and generally better-off) Hindu expenditure – a proxy for income rises – is *not* associated with increases in intercommunal violence. In contrast, a relative increase in (minority and poorer) Muslim expenditure *is* associated with greater violence, showing that improvements in their good fortune are met with hostility against them, but not vice versa. This asymmetry can help one understand the roots and dynamics of violence between Hindus and Muslims and possibly in other conflicts as well. As such, the current research frontier seeks to identify the precise role inequality plays in furthering inter-ethnic violence. Panza and Swee (2020) is an example of such pathbreaking research. Likewise, the question of the intergenerational persistence of inequality is underexplored. Inequality in land or other assets and uneven access to institutional arrangements such as relevant laws and government policies, land titling, property rights, credit access, political representation and taxation, government resource transfers, and fiscal redistributive policies all come into play (Justino and Martorano 2019). In a word, much remains to be explored and understood on a topic that has a long history of exploration within economics.

8.2.2 Twice Victimized? The Forgotten Victims of War

While economists study various macro-developmental and microlevel costs of war, specific victim groups remain understudied. This includes war widows. Between 1985 and 1997, respectively 50 percent and 60 percent of women above the age of sixty were widows in South Asia and Northern Africa (United Nations 2001). Updated estimates show that from 2010 to 2015, war and follow-up diseases increased the rate of widowhood by 9 percent globally and by as much as 24 percent in the Middle East and North Africa (Loomba Foundation 2015). Owing to child or early marriage in poor countries, one in ten women of marriage age is widowed (United Nations 2001). Exceptions notwithstanding (Brück and

Schindler 2009; Owen 2011; Ramnarain 2016), the plight of war widows has received little attention. Essentially absent from the statistics of many developing countries, they are rarely mentioned, even in gender-aware or gender-specific reports on women in war (Loomba Foundation 2015). This is true not only of widows *collectively* but also *individually*, seen for example in their omission in Demography and Health Surveys (DHS), a primary data source on health and well-being in developing countries (Djuikom and van de Walle 2018).

> Where poor countries' men help fight wars or broker peace on behalf of other countries, their wives back home face the risk of widowhood.

A twist on widowhood is that the modern war economy uses many defense contractors from developing countries to work in war zones. At least two dozen countries recruit noncitizens, and in 2003 nearly 33,000 noncitizens served in the US armed forces, valued for their lower attrition, higher retention, and higher promotion rates (O'Neil and Senturk 2004). Even peacekeeping relies on labor from developing countries – approximately 80 percent of UN forces, mostly men.[23] And where poor countries' men help fight wars or broker peace on behalf of other countries, their wives back home face the risk of widowhood. The workers and their families often do not fully know the risks they face, nor the rights technically afforded to them by their employers.[24] Existing research neglects other overlooked groups afflicted by the vagaries of war, such as ethnic or other minorities (for example, Iraqi Yazidis, abused migrant workers), war orphans, the elderly, the disabled, those in detention, the stayers (those who are too poor or disconnected to flee harsh conditions), and the vast number of stateless people. It would help if researchers shifted their focus and studied people, not nations or borders. This is consistent with the principle of methodological individualism at the core of the economic way of thinking. The call here is to fuse conflict, migration, displacement, and other studies with, for example, the foreign and humanitarian aid literature, to expand the scope of within- and cross-border humanitarian assistance and development policies.

8.2.3 Unknown Perpetrators, Nonstate Actors, and Nonwar Wars

Combing through lists of perpetrators in conflict and war statistics, Anderton (2018) noted a substantial increase in the category capturing nonstate actors and also in the "unidentified" actors category. Likewise, Anderton and Brauer

---

[23] http://visionofhumanity.org/peace/eight-facts-about-united-nations-peacekeeping-in-todays-world/.

[24] See, for example, the case of Nepali deaths in US war zones at https://kathmandupost.com/national/2020/08/31/cheap-nepali-deaths-in-us-war-zones.

(forthcoming) sort through ACLED's conflict and location events data set for 1989–2018, finding that unidentified perpetrators accounted for 32 percent of attacks against unarmed civilians and 16 percent of the fatalities caused, and nonstate actors (rebels and militias) account for an additional combined 49 and 68 percent, respectively. Identified *state* actors accounted for the remaining 19 and 16 percentage points, putting numbers on the point that the very nature of organized violence appears to have changed away from overt state involvement.

Relatedly, entire jurisdictional entities and their economies have fallen into a "nonwar war" category, meaning persistent war-level fatalities in countries not "officially" at war. Take Central America – Belize, Costa Rica, El Salvador, Guatemala, Honduras, Nicaragua, and Panama – as a regional example. They score on par with Central and South Asian countries on the Human Development Index (HDI), yet all seven also place within the top-twenty most income-unequal countries worldwide and, for decades, regional homicide rates have been among the very highest in the world (Table 2).[25] Along with other countries – Mexico's illicit narcotics-related violence comes to mind – their "peacetime" violence fatalities exceed the usual threshold rates for war in international statistics (Hoeffler 2018; Anderton and Carter 2019, pp. 9–11). Perhaps more astounding still is that mass atrocities and even genocides occur with some frequency in nation-states otherwise thought to be "at peace" (Anderton and Brauer forthcoming).

While the Human Development Index scores for the seven Central American nation-states are comparable to those of Central and South Asian states, all are among the top-twenty countries with the world's highest income-inequality scores, and their homicide rates likewise are among the very highest in the world.

As a consequence of its non-war war, one-fifth of El Salvador's population (1.4 million people) are migrants. Guatemalans likewise have left in droves, and in 2018 their earnings remittances supported approximately 30 percent of the left-behind population. For Honduras, remittances were approximately 18 percent of its GDP in 2011.[26] Only a few studies analyze the negative externalities of societal violence in the region (Chamarbagwala and Morán 2011; Soares 2015; Melnikov, Schmidt-Padilla, and Sviatschi 2020) and the long-term effects

---

[25] The situation, including levels of violence, is even worse in Pacific Islands Forum states (Brauer 2016) and, more generally, in Small Island Developing States such as the Comoro Islands, Haiti, and the Seychelles (http://unohrlls.org/about-sids/). Conflict and peace economists rarely pay attention to these countries.

[26] Statistics for Guatemala, El Salvador, and Honduras are taken, respectively, from Jonas (2013), Menjívar and Cervantes (2018), and Reichman (2013).

Table 2 Various economic and peace indicators for Central America[a]

Country	2018 Human Development Index (HDI) Rank	Income Share by Top 10% (2014 World Rank)	Average Homicide Rate per 100,000 Population	2020 Global Peace Index Rank (out of 163)
Belize	103	n/a	32.07	n/a
Costa Rica	68	36.9 (11)	7.85	32
El Salvador	124	32.2 (17)	74.18	113
Guatemala	126	38 (9)	33.25	115
Honduras	132	38.1(8)	47.89	119
Nicaragua	126	37.2 (10)	12.76	135
Panama	67	38.5 (7)	11.61	56
Comparable to[b]	(Except Costa Rica and Panama) Kyrgyzstan, Iraq, Palestine, Tajikistan, India, Namibia, Bhutan, and Bangladesh	Ecuador, Comoros, Dominican Republic, Colombia, Brazil, Paraguay, Mexico, Bolivia, Cameroon, Peru, and Russian Federation	South Africa (42.38), Jamaica (40.82), Venezuela (36.43), Brazil (23.76), Puerto Rico (23.16), Mexico (16.09), and Seychelles (11.68)	(Except Costa Rica and Panama) Brazil, Colombia, Mexico, Chad, Myanmar, India, and Mauritania

[a] The latest HDI data pertains to 2018 and is available at http://hdr.undp.org/en/content/human-development-index-hdi. Inequality data obtained through World Bank, Development Research Group database, available at https://data.worldbank.org/indicator/SI.DST.10TH.10. The year 2014 is chosen because it is the latest year for which information on all countries is available. Homicide data obtained from the UNODC, available at https://dataunodc.un.org/content/data/homicide/homicide-rate. The worldwide data is available from the 1990s–2015 or so. The coverage varies for different countries. Average homicide is obtained by averaging the homicide rates across the available years. Global Peace Index data is from the Vision of Humanity. It is available at http://visionofhumanity.org/indexes/global-peace-index/.

[b] Comparison countries, are based on similar rankings of other countries. They are for illustration purposes only and not meant to be a side-by-side and comprehensive comparison.

of the reception, integration, and return of asylum seekers in the United States to Central America (Kalsi 2018). This paucity reflects, in part, a corresponding paucity of large-scale microlevel data sets. Table 3, showing household and microlevel data availability from important data sources, demonstrates how outdated the data are, if available at all. Outdatedness is important, given the youth-oriented age profile of the populations. Also lacking are consistent and detailed statistics on gang membership, internally displaced people (IDPs), human smuggling networks, transmigration, and asylum seekers in neighboring countries. The fluidity of forms of violence across scholars' conceptual borders of war and peace is disconcerting. Economists might do well to cross those borders and focus on the adverse short- and long-term effects of violence, regardless of the labels used.

8.2.4 Law, Society, and Economy

Economics can provide insight into how existing and potential laws stifle, encourage, or change behavior (Brauer, Anderton, and Schap 2016; Brauer, Montolio, and Trujillo-Baute 2016). This includes understanding frictions in political processes that may lead to ineffective enforcement of even well-designed laws in liberal democracies which can suffer from information asymmetries, whereby parties tasked with checking opportunism lack access to the information necessary to effectively carry out their role. Information asymmetries are magnified in the national security state where secrecy and the (over) classification of information in the name of national security is the norm. Skewed incentives arise and, to conceal opportunistic behavior, the monitored people can shape what information flows to its overseers. This results in significant slack in the existing rules meant to limit the abuse of power.

Economists can analyze the incentives created by various institutional arrangements and their impact on the effectiveness of law. They also can offer potential solutions. For example, economists have highlighted that whistle-blowing can be understood as a mechanism for resolving information asymmetries in democratic politics (Coyne, Goodman, and Hall 2019). This *economic* explanation is distinct from legal or ethical studies of whistleblowing and demonstrates the importance of law and economics for identifying mechanisms to check the abuse of state power.

8.3 Conclusion: An Institutional Approach for Stable Peace

Economics can help design well-functioning governance institutions, and conflict and peace economics is no exception to this. An attainable task of conflict and peace economics regards the design and functioning of political, economic,

Table 3 Central America household and micro-data availability from key data sources[a]

Country	Demographic and Health Survey (DHS) Data	Integrated Public Use Microdata Series (IPUMS), International	World Value Survey (WVS)	World Bank Living Standard Measurement Study (LSMS)
Belize	No data available	No data available	No data available	No data available
Costa Rica	No data available	1963, 1973, 1984, 2000, 2011	No data available	No data available
El Salvador	1985	1992 and 2007	1999	No data available
Guatemala	1987, 1995, 1997 (in depth), 1998–1999 (interim), 2014–2015, and 2020	1964, 1973, 1981, 1994, 2002	2004 and 2009	2000
Honduras	2005–2006 and 2011–2012	1961, 1974, 1988, and 2001	No data available	No data available
Nicaragua	1998 and 2001	1971, 1995, and 2005	2019	1993, 1998–1999, 2001, and 2005
Panama	No data available	1960, 1970, 1980, 1990, 2000, 2010	No data available	1997, 2003, and 2008

[a] DHS data is available at https://dhsprogram.com/, IPUMS at https://international.ipums.org/international-action/samples, WVS at www.worldvalues survey.org/wvs.jsp, and LSMS at https://microdata.worldbank.org/index.php/catalog/lsms.

and cultural institutions for peaceful and irreversibly stable societies. The literature is lopsided in that it still is more about violence and war than it is about nonviolence and peace. Studying why auction markets fail, for example, is not the same thing as studying how they may succeed. Indeed, a series of economics Nobel Prize awards have in recent years recognized economists' constructive contributions in approaching some of the greatest problems of our times. Shifting our focus to peace economics provides a means of appreciating and studying institutions to understand the factors that contribute to peace rather than to (violent) conflict.

> An attainable task for conflict and peace economics regards the design and functioning of political, economic, and cultural institutions for peaceful, stable societies.

One example of such an approach is Boulding's (1978) classification of characteristics of social systems into two related groups, strength and strain, where strength is the ability to resist breakage under strain. Figure 3 shows strength *relative to* strain. Changes in one relative to the other can then lead to phase transitions (Figure 4). This conceptualization is useful for understanding the movement of societies from war to peace (or vice versa) and in creating institutions that can help societies remain in the stable peace zone. Brauer and Dunne (2012) outline institutional design criteria to promote peace. Besley and Persson (2011) further frame state institutions, absence of political violence, and high per-capita income as three pillars of prosperity. Studies like these, and case studies accompanying the conceptual instruments, still are all too rare.

Section 8.2.4 discussed how economists are well positioned to study laws, the incentives they create, and potential institutional arrangements that can facilitate

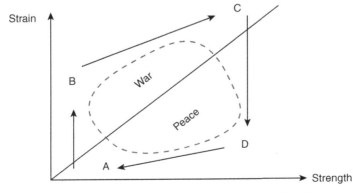

Figure 3 Strain versus strength in Boulding (1978).

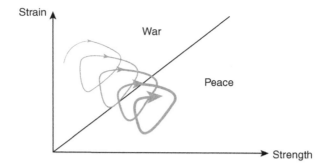

Figure 4 Movement from stable war to stable peace in Boulding (1978).

better societal outcomes. At the same time, Section 6 outlined some challenges in postwar reconstruction policies. Combining these serves as a reminder of our capacity to do both good and harm (Coyne 2013). As such, a repeatedly appearing theme is the need to recognize both advancements in our understanding of the world *and* the constraint on human knowledge to design the world as "the experts" envision. Indeed, efforts to design institutions have often contributed to conflict – think of "civilized colonization" or more recent "nation building" efforts, such as in Afghanistan and Iraq. Academics and policy makers alike benefit from humility and the recognition of "negative knowledge" (Viner 1950) – knowledge of the things we do not know and how a lack of knowledge serves as a constraint on what is possible in institutional design and reform.

Nobel Laureate Elinor Ostrom, the first female to be awarded the economics prize, studied influential models of collective action where individual interests clash with the common good. While appreciating their value as analytical frameworks, Ostrom took issue with social scientists' tendency to treat models as if they were, always and everywhere, reflective of reality (Ostrom 1990). The theory of collective action, she noted, was really a theory of collective *in*action because the people in the game are assumed to be passive pawns who simply respond to given rules and payoffs. Ostrom's contribution was to highlight that people do not live in a world of predetermined and fixed rules and payoffs. Instead, human beings are creative and entrepreneurial and possess the ability to strategize about and change the world in which they live. This provides a reason for hope because it suggests that people have the power to transform situations of conflict into situations of peaceful cooperation that contribute to human well-being.

References

Adams, Karen Ruth. 2003/4. "Attack and Conquer? International Anarchy and the Offense-Defense Deterrence Balance." *International Security* 28(3): 45–83.

Akerlof, George A. 2020. "Sins of Omission and the Practice of Economics." *Journal of Economic Literature* 58(2): 405–18.

Anderson, William L., Scott A. Kjar, and James D. Yohe. 2012. "War and the Austrian School: Modern Austrian Economists Take on Aggressive Wars." *The Economics of Peace and Security Journal* 7(1): 30–7.

Anderton, Charles H. 2003. "Economic Theorizing of Conflict: Historical Contributions, Future Possibilities." *Defence and Peace Economics* 14(3): 209–22.

2018. "Subterranean Atrocities: A Twenty-First Century Challenge for Mass Atrocity Prevention." In *Last Lectures on the Prevention and Intervention of Genocide*, Samuel Totten (ed.), 163–70. New York: Routledge.

Anderton, Charles H., and Roxane A. Anderton. 1997. "The Economics of Conflict, Production, and Exchange." In *Economics of Conflict and Peace*, Jurgen Brauer and William G. Gissy (eds.), 54–82. Aldershot: Avebury.

Anderton, Charles H., and Jurgen Brauer. 2016. "Genocide and Mass Killing Risk and Prevention: Perspectives from Constrained Optimization Models." In *Economic Aspects of Genocides, Other Mass Atrocities, and Their Prevention*, Charles H. Anderton and Jurgen Brauer (eds.), 143–71. New York: Oxford University Press.

Forthcoming. "Mass Atrocities and Their Prevention." *Journal of Economic Literature*.

Anderton, Charles H., and John R. Carter. 2019. *Principles of Conflict Economics: The Political Economy of War, Terrorism, Genocide, and Peace*, 2nd ed. New York: Cambridge University Press.

Baran, Paul A. 1957. *The Political Economy of Growth*. New York: Monthly Review Press.

Bas, Muhammet, and Robert Schub. 2016. "Mutual Optimism as a Cause of Conflict: Secret Alliances and Conflict Onset." *International Studies Quarterly* 60(3): 552–64.

Bazley, Tom. 2010. *Crimes of the Art World*. Santa Barbara: Praeger.

Becker, Gary S. 1968. "Crime and Punishment: An Economic Approach." *Journal of Political Economy* 76(2): 169–217.

Bell, Sam R., and Jesse C. Johnson. 2015. "Shifting Power, Commitment Problems, and Preventive War." *International Studies Quarterly* 59(1): 124–32.

Besley, Timothy, and Torsten Persson. 2011. *Pillars of Prosperity: The Political Economics of Development Clusters.* New Jersey: Princeton University Press.

Beyer, Anna Cornelia. 2018. "Abolishing the Security Dilemma: Why We Need to Integrate the Militaries." *Cambridge Journal of Eurasian Studies* 2(1): 1–20.

Blattman, Christopher, and Edward Miguel. 2010. "Civil War." *Journal of Economic Literature* 48(1): 3–57.

Böhm-Bawerk, Eugen von. 1889 [1959]. "The Positive Theory of Capital." In *Capital and Interest,* vol. 2. South Holland: Libertarian Press.

Boulding, Kenneth E. 1945. *The Economics of Peace.* New York: Prentice Hall.

1962. *Conflict and Defense.* New York: Harpers.

1978. *Stable Peace.* Austin: University of Texas Press.

Boulding, Kenneth E., Martin Pfaff, and Janos Horvath. 1972. "Grants Economics: A Simple Introduction." *The American Economist* 16(1): 19–28.

Bozzoli, Carlos, Tilman Brück, and Simon Sottsas. 2010. "A Survey of the Global Economic Costs of Conflict." *Defence and Peace Economics* 21(2): 165–76.

Brauer, Jurgen. 2007a. "Review of V.W. Ruttan's 'Is War Necessary for Economic Growth?'" *Economic Development and Cultural Change* 55(3): 627–30.

2007b. "Review Article: Is War Necessary for Economic Growth?" *The Economics of Peace and Security Journal* 2(1): 71–6.

2016. "Rethinking Development in the Pacific Islands Forum Countries." *International Journal of Development and Conflict* 6(1): 47–60.

2017. "'On the Expence of Defence': What Have We Learned Since Adam Smith?" *Peace Economics, Peace Science and Public Policy* 23(2): Art. 1.

2019. "Don't Just Click 'Download': The Case of U.S. Military Expenditure Data." *The Economics of Peace and Security Journal* 14(2): 55–64.

Brauer, Jurgen, and Charles H. Anderton. 2020. "Conflict and Peace Economics: Retrospective and Prospective Reflections on Concepts, Theories, and Data." *Defence and Peace Economics* 31(4): 443–65.

Brauer, Jurgen, Charles H. Anderton, and David Schap. 2016. "Genocides and Other Mass Atrocities: A Law and Economics Approach." In *Economic Aspects of Genocides, Other Mass Atrocities, and Their Prevention,*

Charles H. Anderton and Jurgen Brauer (eds.), 639–62. New York: Oxford University Press.

Brauer, Jurgen, and Raul Caruso. 2013. "Economists and Peacebuilding." In *Handbook of Peacebuilding*, Roger MacGinty (ed.), 147–58. London: Routledge.

Brauer, Jurgen, and J. Paul Dunne. 2012. *Peace Economics: A Macroeconomic Primer for Violence-Afflicted States*. Washington, DC: United States Institute of Peace.

Brauer, Jurgen, J. Paul Dunne, and Nan Tian. 2019. "Towards Demilitarisation? The Military Expenditure – Development Nexus Revisited." In *The Political Economy of Defense*, Ron Matthews (ed.), 90–117. Cambridge: Cambridge University Press.

Brauer, Jurgen, and Topher McDougal. 2020. "Bioeconomic Peace Research and Policy." *Peace Economics, Peace Science and Public Policy* 26(3): 1–9.

Brauer, Jurgen, Daniel Montolio, and Elisa Trujillo-Baute. 2016. "How Do US State Firearms Laws Affect Firearms Manufacturing Location? An Empirical Investigation, 1986–2010." *Journal of Economic Geography* 17(4): 753–90.

Braun, Robert. 2019. *Protectors of Pluralism: Religious Minorities and the Rescue of Jews in the Low Countries during the Holocaust*. New York: Cambridge University Press.

Brewer, Tony. 2002. *Marxist Theories of Imperialism: A Critical Survey*, 2nd ed. New York: Routledge.

Brück, Tilman. 2001. War and Underdevelopment: Volume 1: The Economic and Social Consequences of Conflict, Frances Stewart, Valpy FitzGerald, and Associates (eds.), 56–88. Oxford: Oxford University Press.

2005. "An Economic Analysis of Security Policies." *Defence and Peace Economics* 16(5): 375–89.

Brück, Tilman, and Kati Schindler. 2009. "The Impact of Violent Conflicts on Households: What Do We Know and What Should We Know about War Widows?" *Oxford Development Studies* 37(3): 289–309.

Brzoska, Michael. 1983. "Research Communication: The Military Related External Debt of Third World Countries." *Journal of Peace Research* 20 (3): 271–7.

Brzoska, Michael, and Christiane Fröhlich. 2016. "Climate Change, Migration and Violent Conflict: Vulnerabilities, Pathways and Adaptation Strategies." *Migration and Development* 5(2): 190–210.

Buchanan, James M. 1975. *The Limits of Liberty: Between Anarchy and Leviathan*. Chicago: University of Chicago Press.

Case, Anne, and Angus Deaton. 1987. *Analysis of Household Expenditures.* Washington, DC: The World Bank.

Chamarbagwala, Rubiana, and Hilcías E. Morán. 2011. "The Human Capital Consequences of Civil War: Evidence from Guatemala." *Journal of Development Economics* 94(1): 41–61.

Chamlee-Wright, Emily, and Virgil Henry Storr. 2011. "Social Capital as Collective Narratives and Post-Disaster Community Recovery." *Sociological Review* 59(2): 266–82.

Cole, David, and James X. Dempsey. 2006. *Terrorism and the Constitution: Sacrificing Civil Liberties in the Name of National Security.* New York: The New Press.

Cole, David, and Jules Lobel. 2009. *Less Safe, Less Free: Why America Is Losing the War on Terror.* New York: The New Press.

Collier, Paul. 1999. "On the Economic Consequences of Civil War." *Oxford Economic Papers* 51(1): 168–83.

Collier, Paul, and Anke Hoeffler. 2004. "Greed and Grievance in Civil War." *Oxford Economic Papers* 56(4): 563–95.

Cornes, Richard, and Todd Sandler. 1984. "Easy Riders, Joint Production, and Public Goods." *Economic Journal* 94(375): 580–98.

Coulomb, Fanny, 2004. *Economic Theories of Peace and War.* London: Routledge.

Coulomb, Fanny, and J. Paul Dunne. 2008. "Peace, War and International Security: Economic Theories." In *War, Peace, and Security,* Jacques Fontanel and Manas Chatterji (eds.), 13–36. Bingley: Emerald.

Coyne, Christopher J. 2013. *Doing Bad by Doing Good: Why Humanitarian Action Fails.* Stanford: Stanford University Press.

2015. "Lobotomizing the Defense Brain." *Review of Austrian Economics* 28(4): 371–96.

2020. *Defense, Peace, and War Economics.* Elements in Austrian Economics. Cambridge: Cambridge University Press.

Coyne, Christopher J., and Brittany L. Bills. 2018. "Overlooked Costs of War-Related Public Research." *The Independent Review: A Journal of Political Economy* 22(3): 429–34.

Coyne, Christopher J., and Anne R. Bradley. 2019. "Ludwig von Mises on War and the Economy." *Review of Austrian Economics* 32(3): 215–28.

Coyne, Christopher J., Nathan Goodman, and Abigail R. Hall. 2019. "Sounding the Alarm: The Political Economy of Whistleblowing in the US Security State." *Peace Economics, Peace Science and Public Policy* 25(1): 1–11.

Coyne, Christopher J., and Abigail R. Hall. 2014. "Perfecting Tyranny: Foreign Intervention as Experimentation in State Control." *The Independent Review: A Journal of Political Economy* 19(2): 1–25.

2018. *Tyranny Comes Home: The Domestic Fate of US Militarism*. Stanford: Stanford University Press.

Craft, Cassady B. 2000. "An Analysis of the Washington Naval Agreements and the Economic Provisions of Arms Control Theory." *Defence and Peace Economics* 11(1): 127–48.

Cramer, Christopher. 2006. *Civil War Is Not a Stupid Thing: Accounting for Violence in Developing Countries*. London: Hurst & Company.

Cypher, James M. 2008. "Economic Consequences of Armaments Production: Institutional Perspectives of JK Galbraith and TB Veblen." *Journal of Economic Issues* 42(1): 37–49.

d'Agostino, Giorgio, J. Paul Dunne, and Luca Pieroni. 2016. "Government Spending, Corruption and Economic Growth." *World Development* 84 (August): 190–205.

Dixit, Avinash K., Susan Skeath, and David H. Reiley Jr. 2014. *Games of Strategy*, 4th ed. New York: W. W. Norton & Company.

Djuikom, M. A., and D. van de Walle. 2018. *Marital Shocks and Women's Welfare in Africa*. Washington, DC: The World Bank.

Duncan, Thomas K., and Christopher J. Coyne. 2013. "The Overlooked Costs of the Permanent War Economy: A Market Process Approach." *Review of Austrian Economics* 26(4): 413–31.

Dunne, J. Paul. 1995. "The Defense Industrial Base." In *Handbook of Defense Economics*, vol. 1, Keith Hartley and Todd Sandler (eds.), 399–430. New York: Elsevier.

1996. "Economic Effects of Military Expenditure in Developing Countries: A Survey." In *The Peace Dividend*, N. P. Gleditsch, A. Cappelen, O. Bjerkholt, R. P. Smith, and J. P. Dunne (eds.), 439–64. Bingley: Emerald Group Publishing.

2006. "After the Slaughter: Reconstructing Mozambique and Rwanda." *The Economics of Peace and Security Journal* 1(2): 39–46.

2013. "Armed Conflicts." In *Global Problems, Smart Solutions: Costs and Benefits*, Bjorn Lomborg (ed.), 21–53. Cambridge: Cambridge University Press.

2017. "War, Peace, and Development." *The Economics of Peace and Security Journal* 12(2): 21–31.

Dunne, J. Paul, Sam Perlo-Freeman, and Aylin Soydan. 2004. "Military Expenditure and Debt in South America." *Defence and Peace Economics* 15(2): 173–87.

Dunne, J. Paul, and Ron P. Smith. 2020. "Military Expenditure, Investment and Growth." *Defence and Peace Economics* 31(6): 601–14.

Dunne, J. Paul, Ron P. Smith, and Dirk Willenbockel. 2005. "Models of Military Expenditure and Growth: A Critical Review." *Defence and Peace Economics* 16(6): 449–61.

Dunne, J. Paul, and Nan Tian. 2013. "Military Expenditure and Economic Growth: A Survey." *The Economics of Peace and Security Journal* 8(1): 5–11.

2015. "Military Expenditure, Economic Growth and Heterogeneity." *Defence and Peace Economics* 26(1): 15–31.

2019. "Conflict Determinants in Africa." *The Economics of Peace and Security Journal* 14(2): 21–31.

2020. "Military Expenditures and Economic Growth." In *Oxford Research Encyclopedia of Politics*. Oxford: Oxford University Press.

Dziubiński, Marcin, Sanjeev Goyal, and Adrien Vigier. 2016. "Conflict and Networks." In *The Oxford Handbook of the Economics of Networks*, Yann Bramoullé, Andrea Galeotti, and Brian Rogers (eds.), 215–43. New York: Oxford University Press.

Elveren, Adem Yavuz. 2019. *The Economics of Military Spending: A Marxist Perspective*. New York: Routledge.

Enders, Walter, and Paan Jindapon. 2010. "Network Externalities and the Structure of Terror Networks." *Journal of Conflict Resolution* 54(2): 262–80.

Enders, Walter, and Todd Sandler. 2000. "Is Transnational Terrorism Becoming More Threatening?" *Journal of Conflict Resolution* 44(3): 307–32.

2012. *The Political Economy of Terrorism*, 2nd ed. New York: Cambridge University Press.

Fearon, James D. 1995. "Rationalist Explanations for War." *International Organization* 49(3): 379–414.

Fearon, James D., and David D. Laitin. 2003. "Ethnicity, Insurgency, and Civil War." *The American Political Science Review* 97(1): 75–90.

Finkel, Evgeny. 2017. *Ordinary Jews: Choice and Survival during the Holocaust*. Princeton, NJ: Princeton University Press.

Gaibulloev, Khusrav, and Todd Sandler. 2019. "What We Have Learned about Terrorism since 9/11." *Journal of Economic Literature* 57(2): 275–328.

Galbraith, James K. 2016. *Inequality: What Everyone Needs to Know*. New York: Oxford University Press.

Ghobarah, Hazem Adam, Paul Huth, and Bruce Russett. 2003. "Civil Wars Kill and Maim People Long after the Shooting Stops." *American Political Science Review* 97(2): 189–202.

Granovetter, Mark. 1978. "Threshold Models of Collective Behavior." *American Journal of Sociology* 83(6): 489–515.

Gray, Kenneth R. 1990. *Soviet Agriculture: Comparative Perspectives*. Ames: Iowa State University Press.

Grossman, Herschel I. 1991. "A General Equilibrium Model of Insurrections." *American Economic Review* 81(4): 912–21.

Harris, Geoff. 1999. *Recovery from Armed Conflict in Developing Countries*. New York: Routledge.

Hartley, Keith. 2020. *Defense Economics: Achievements and Challenges*. Elements in Defense Economics. Cambridge: Cambridge University Press.

Hayek, F. A. 1945. *Individualism and Economic Order*. Chicago: Chicago University Press.

Higgs, Robert. 1987. *Crisis and Leviathan: Critical Episodes in the Growth of American Government*. New York: Oxford University Press.

2006. *Depression, War, and the Cold War*. New York: Oxford University Press.

2012. *Delusions of Power: New Explorations of State, War, and Economy*. Oakland: Independent Institute.

Hirshleifer, Jack. 1983. "From Weakest-Link to Best-Shot: The Voluntary Provision of Public Goods." *Public Choice* 41(3): 371–86.

2001. *The Dark Side of the Force: Economic Foundations of Conflict Theory*. Cambridge: Cambridge University Press.

Hoeffler, Anke. 2018. "Security and Development: Shifting the Focus to Interpersonal Violence." *The Economics of Peace and Security Journal* 13(1): 12–23.

Howard, Michael C., and John E. King. 1989. *A History of Marxian Economics: Volume I, 1883–1929*. Basingstoke: Macmillan International Higher Education.

1992. *A History of Marxian Economics: Volume II: 1929–1990*. Basingstoke: Macmillan International Higher Education.

Hughes, Jonathan R.T. 1977. *The Governmental Habit*. New York: Basic Books.

Institute for Economics and Peace. 2011. "Economic Consequences of War on the US Economy." www.economicsandpeace.org/wp-content/uploads/2015/06/The-Economic-Consequences-of-War-on-US-Economy_0.pdf>.

Intriligator, Michael D. 1975. "Strategic Considerations in the Richardson Model of Arms Races." *Journal of Political Economy* 83(2): 339–54.

Irons, Peter. 2005. *War Powers: How the Imperial Presidency Hijacked the Constitution*. New York: Metropolitan Books.

Jevons, William Stanley. 1866. "Brief Account of a General Mathematical Theory of Political Economy." *Journal of the Royal Statistical Society* 29(June): 282–7.

Jha, Saumitra. 2007. "Maintaining Peace across Ethnic Lines: New Lessons from the Past." *The Economics of Peace and Security Journal* 2(2): 81–93.

Jonas, Susanne. 2013. "Guatemalan Migration in Times of Civil War and Post-War Challenges." www.migrationpolicy.org/article/guatemalan-migration -times-civil-war-and-post-war-challenges.

Justino, Patricia, and Bruno Martorano. 2019. "Redistributive Preferences and Protests in Latin America." *Journal of Conflict Resolution* 63(9): 2128–54.

Kaldor, Mary. 1982. *The Baroque Arsenal*. Harmondsworth: Deutsch.

Kalsi, Priti. 2018. "The Impact of U.S. Deportation of Criminals on Gang Development and Education in El Salvador." *Journal of Development Economics* 135 (November): 433–48.

Kaul, Inge, Isabelle Grunberg, and Marc A. Stern. 1999. "Defining Global Public Goods." In *Global Public Goods: International Cooperation in the 21st Century*, Inge Kaul, Isabelle Grunberg, and Marc A. Stern (eds.), 2–19. New York: United Nations Development Programme.

Kautsky, Karl. 1914. "Der Imperialismus." *Die Neue Zeit*, 11 September 1914, 32(2): 908–22.

Keynes, John M. 1919. *The Economic Consequences of the Peace*. London: Macmillan.

Kidron, Michael. 1967. "A Permanent Arms Economy." *International Socialism* (1st series) No. 28: 8–12. www.marxists.org/archive/kidron/ works/1967/xx/permarms.htm.

Kinne, Brandon J. 2012. "Multilateral Trade and Militarized Conflict: Centrality, Openness, and Asymmetry in the Global Trade Network." *Journal of Politics* 74(1): 308–22.

Kjar, Scott A., and William L. Anderson. 2010. "War and the Austrian School: Applying the Economics of the Founders." *The Economics of Peace and Security Journal* 5(1): 6–11.

König, Michael D., Dominic Rohner, Mathias Thoenig, and Fabrizio Zilibotti. 2017. "Networks in Conflict: Theory and Evidence from the Great War of Africa." *Econometrica* 85(4): 1093–132.

Lachmann, Ludwig. 1956. *Capital and Its Structure*. Kansas City: Sheed, Andrews, and McMeel.

Lange, Oskar. 1936. "On the Economic Theory of Socialism: Part One." *Review of Economic Studies* 4(1): 53–71.

———. 1937. "On the Economic Theory of Socialism: Part Two." *Review of Economic Studies* 4(2): 123–42.

Lerner, Abba. 1934. "Economic Theory and Socialist Economy." *Review of Economic Studies* 2(1): 51–61.

1936. "A Note on Socialist Economics." *Review of Economic Studies* 4(1): 72–6.

1937. "Statics and Dynamics in Socialist Economics." *Economic Journal* 47(186): 253–70.

1938. "Theory and Practice in Socialist Economics." *Review of Economic Studies* 6(1): 71–5.

Linfield, Michael. 1990. *Freedom under Fire: US Civil Liberties in Times of War*. Boston: South End Press.

Loomba Foundation. 2015. "The Global Widows Report 2015: A Global Overview of Deprivation Faced by Widows and Their Children." www.euromedwomen.foundation/pg/en/documents/view/8065/the-glo bal-widows-report-2015-a-global-overview-of-deprivation-faced-by-widows-and-their-children.

Madison, James. 1865. "Political Observations, April 20, 1795." In *Letters and Other Writings of James Madison*, vol. 4, 485–505. Philadelphia: J. B. Lippincott & Co.

Maoz, Zeev. 2011. *Networks of Nations: The Evolution, Structure, and Impact of International Networks, 1816–2011*. New York: Cambridge University Press.

McCloskey, Donald N. 1983. "The Rhetoric of Economics." *Journal of Economic Literature* 21(2): 481–517.

McDoom, Omar S. 2013. "Who Killed in Rwanda's Genocide? Micro-Space, Social Influence and Individual Participation in Intergroup Violence." *Journal of Peace Research* 50(4): 453–67.

Melman, Seymour. 1970. *Pentagon Capitalism: The Political Economy of War*. New York: McGraw-Hill.

1974. *The Permanent War Economy: American Capitalism in Decline*. New York: Simon and Schuster.

Melnikov, Nikita, Carlos Schmidt-Padilla, and Maria Micaela Sviatschi. 2020. "Gangs, Labor Mobility and Development." National Bureau of Economic Research Working Paper no. w27832.

Menjívar, Cecilia, and Andrea Gómez Cervantes. 2018. "El Salvador: Civil War, Natural Disasters, and Gang Violence Drive Migration." www.migra tionpolicy.org/article/el-salvador-civil-war-natural-disasters-and-gang-violence-drive-migration.

Mises, Ludwig von. 1919 [2006]. *Nation, State, and Economy: Contributions to the Politics and History of Our Time*. Indianapolis:Liberty Fund.

1920 [1935]. "Economic Calculation in the Socialist Commonwealth." In *Collectivist Economic Planning*, F. A. Hayek (ed.), 87–130. Clifton, NJ: Augustus M. Kelley.

1922 [1981]. *Socialism: An Economic and Sociological Analysis.* Indianapolis: Liberty Fund.

1949. *Human Action: A Treatise on Economics.* Chicago: Henry Regnery.

Mitra, Anirban, and Debraj Ray. 2014. "Implications of an Economic Theory of Conflict: Hindu-Muslim Violence in India." *Journal of Political Economy* 122(4): 719–65.

Moscona, Jacob, Nathan Nunn, and James A. Robinson. 2020. "Segmentary Lineage Organization and Conflict in Sub-Saharan Africa." *Econometrica* 88(5): 1999–2036.

Narang, Neil. 2015. "Assisting Uncertainty: How Humanitarian Aid Can Inadvertently Prolong Civil War." *International Studies Quarterly* 59(1): 184–95.

Neurath, Otto. 1919 [1973]. "Through War Economy to Economy in Kind." In *Otto Neurath: Empiricism and Sociology*, Vienna Circle Collection, vol. 1, Mary Neurath and Robert S. Cohen (eds.), 123–57. Dordrecht, Holland: D. Reidel Publishing Company.

Nunn, Nathan, and Leonard Wantchekon. 2011. "The Slave Trade and the Origins of Mistrust in Africa." *American Economic Review* 101(7): 3221–52.

Olson, Mancur, and Richard Zeckhauser. 1966. "An Economic Theory of Alliances." *Review of Economics and Statistics* 48(3): 266–79.

O'Neil, Lynn G., and Omer S. Senturk. 2004. *Noncitizens in the US Military.* Monterey, CA: Naval Postgraduate School.

Ostrom, Elinor. 1990. *Governing the Commons: The Evolution of Institutions for Collective Action.* New York: Cambridge University Press.

Owen, Margaret. 2011. "Widowhood Issues in the Context of United Nations Security Council Resolution 1325." *International Feminist Journal of Politics* 13(4): 616–22.

Panza, Laura, and Eik Swee. 2020. "Inter-Ethnic Income Inequality and Conflict Intensification in Mandate Palestine." http://dx.doi.org/10.2139/ssrn.3079236.

Peacock, Allan T., and Jack Wiseman. 1961. *The Growth of Public Expenditure in the United Kingdom.* Princeton, NJ: Princeton University Press.

Peck, Merton J., and Frederic M. Scherer. 1962. *The Weapons Acquisition Process: An Economic Analysis.* Boston: Harvard University Press.

Peltzman, Sam. 1980. "The Growth of Government." *Journal of Law & Economics* 23(2): 209–87.

Piketty, Thomas. 2015. *The Economics of Inequality.* Boston: Harvard University Press.

Pivetti, Massimo. 1992. "Military Spending as a Burden on Growth: An Underconsumptionist' Critique." *Cambridge Journal of Economics* 16(4): 373–84.

1994. "Effective Demand, Marxo-Marginalism, and the Economics of Military Spending: A Rejoinder." *Cambridge Journal of Economics* 18(5): 523–27.

Porter, Bruce D. 1980. "Parkinson's Law Revisited: War and the Growth of American Government." *The Public Interest* 60: 50–68.

1994. *War and the Rise of the State: The Military Foundations of Modern Politics*. New York: The Free Press.

Ramnarain, Smita. 2016. "Unpacking Widow Headship and Agency in Post-Conflict Nepal." *Feminist Economics* 22(1): 80–105.

Rehnquist, William H. 1998. *All The Laws but One: Civil Liberties in Wartime*. New York: Vintage Books.

Reichman, D. 2013. "Honduras: The Perils of Remittance Dependence and Clandestine Migration." www.migrationpolicy.org/article/honduras-perils-remittance-dependence-and-clandestine-migration.

Rockoff, Hugh. 1999. "World War II and the Growth of the U.S. Federal Government." *Japan and the World Economy* 11(2): 245–62.

Ruttan, Vernon W. 2006. *Is War Necessary for Economic Growth? Military Procurement and Technology Development*. New York: Oxford University Press.

Sambanis, Nicholas. 2002. "A Review of Recent Advances and Future Directions in the Quantitative Literature on Civil War." *Defence and Peace Economics* 13(3): 215–43.

Samuelson, Paul. 1954. "The Pure Theory of Public Expenditure." *Review of Economics and Statistics* 36(4): 387–9.

1955. "Diagrammatic Exposition of a Theory of Public Expenditure." *Review of Economics and Statistics* 37(4): 350–6.

Sandler, Todd. 1999. Global Public Goods: International Cooperation in the 21st Century, Inge Kaul, Isabelle Grunberg, and Marc A. Stern (eds.), 20–50. New York: Oxford University Press.

Sandler, Todd, and Kevin Siqueira. 2009. "Games and Terrorism." *Simulation & Gaming* 40(2): 164–92.

Sarntisart, Isra. 2020. "Income Inequality and Conflicts: A Gini Decomposition Analysis." *The Economics of Peace and Security Journal* 15(2): 66–82.

Schelling, Thomas C. 1978. *Micromotives and Macrobehavior*. New York: W. W. Norton.

Schlesinger, Arthur M. Jr. 2004. *The Imperial Presidency*. Boston: Mariner Books.

Sen, Amartya M., and James E. Foster. 1997. *On Economic Inequality.* New York: Oxford University Press.

Sheehan, Nadège. 2011. *The Economics of UN Peacekeeping.* New York: Routledge.

Shiller, Robert J. 2017. "Narrative Economics." *American Economic Review* 107(4): 967–1004.

Silwal, Shikha. 2013. "A Spatial-Temporal Analysis of Civil War: The Case of Nepal." *The Economics of Peace and Security Journal* 8(2): 20–5.

2017. "On Peace and Development Economics." *The Economics of Peace and Security Journal* 12(2): 5–9.

2021. "Looting and Destruction of Cultural Heritage Objects through an Economic Lens." Working Paper available at SSRN: https://ssrn.com/abstract=3739452 or http://dx.doi.org/10.2139/ssrn.3739452

Smith, Ron P. 1977. "Military Expenditure and Capitalism." *Cambridge Journal of Economics* 1(1): 61–76.

2000. "Defence Expenditure and Economic Growth." In *Making Peace Pay: A Bibliography on Disarmament and Conversion,* Nils Petter Gleditsch, Goran Lindgren, Naima Mouhleb, Sjoerd Smit, and Indra De Soysa (eds.), 15–24. Claremont, CA:Regina Books.

2011. *Military Economics: The Interaction of Power and Money.* New York: Palgrave Macmillan.

2014. "The Economic Costs of Military Conflict." *Journal of Peace Research* 51(2): 245–56.

2020. "Debt, Deficits and Defence: The UK Experience 1700–2016." *Defence and Peace Economics* 31(4): 414–22.

Smith, Ron P., and J. Paul Dunne. 1994. "Is Military Spending a Burden? A Marxo-Marginalist Response to Pivetti." *Cambridge Journal of Economics* 18(5): 515–21.

Soares, Rodrigo R. 2015. "Welfare Costs of Crime and Common Violence." *Journal of Economic Studies* 42(1): 117–37.

Stewart, Frances. 2016. *Horizontal Inequalities and Conflict: Understanding Group Violence in Multiethnic Societies.* New York: Springer.

Streek, Wolfgang. 2020. "Engel's Second Theory: Technology, Warfare and the Growth of the State." *New Left Review* 123: 75–88.

Swee, Eik. 2016. "Economics of Civil War." *Australian Economic Review* 49(1): 105–11.

Toporowski, Jan. 2017. "Kalecki on Technology and Military Keynesianism." https://papers.ssrn.com/sol3/papers.cfm?abstract_id=3063914.

Trapeznikova, Ija. 2019. "Measuring Income Inequality." *IZA World of Labor.* doi: 10.15185/izawol.462.

Tussing, A. Dale, and John A. Henning. 1974. "Long-Run Growth of Nondefense Government Expenditures in the United States." *Public Finance Quarterly* 2(2): 202–22.

United Nations. 2001. "Women2000: Widowhood: Invisible Women, Secluded or Excluded." www.unwomen.org/en/digital-library/publications/2001/12/women2000-widowhood-invisible-women-secluded-or-excluded.

Verwimp, Philip, Patricia Justino, and Tilman Brück. 2019. "The Microeconomics of Violent Conflict." *Journal of Development Economics* 141: 1–6.

Viner, Jacob. 1950. "A Modest Proposal for Some Stress on Scholarship in Graduate Training. Address before the Graduate Convocation, Brown University, June 3, 1950." *Brown University Papers* 24. Providence: Brown University.

Walker, Samuel. 2012. *Presidents and Civil Liberties from Wilson to Obama: A Story of Poor Custodians.* New York: Cambridge University Press.

Waller, James. 2007. *Becoming Evil: How Ordinary People Commit Genocide and Mass Killing*, 2nd ed. New York: Oxford University Press.

Westley, Christopher, William L. Anderson, and Scott A. Kjar. 2011. "War and the Austrian School: Ludwig von Mises and Friedrich von Hayek." *The Economics of Peace and Security Journal* 6(1): 28–33.

Wilson, Maya, David R. Davis, and Amanda Murdie. 2016. "The View from the Bottom." *Journal of Peace Research* 53(3): 442–58.

Acknowledgements

Silwal is grateful for sabbatical support from a Lenfest Grant awarded by Washington and Lee University. She is also thankful to the Economics Department for a Morris Teaching Grant that supported numerous revisions of her Economics of War and Peace course, and to the students in her Economics of War and Peace class for their engagement and interest in this topic.

With gratefulness to my wife, Roxane, for her bountiful encouragement, to my sons and daughter-in-law, Mark, James, and Sarah, for their love, and to my department colleagues for their unsparing support. – CA

With gratitude to Jennifer Salamanca-Brauer for her understanding and support and to the colleagues I have had the fortune and joy to work with over the years. – JB

To students dedicated to the study of conflict and the search for peace. – CC

To my father John Dunne and the memory of my mother, Mary. – JPD

To my parents, Shiba B. Basnet and Binita Pant Basnet, for their love and care, and to Dr. Rupesh Silwal for his companionship and understanding. – SS

About the Authors

Charles H. Anderton is Professor of Economics and Distinguished Professor of Ethics and Society, College of the Holy Cross, Worcester, MA, USA. He is the author or coauthor of numerous peer-reviewed articles and several books and associate editor of *The Economics of Peace and Security Journal*. His recent work, with Jurgen Brauer, focuses on the economics of mass atrocities and their prevention.

Jurgen Brauer is Visiting Professor, Faculty of Economics, Chulalongkorn University, Bangkok, Thailand, and Emeritus Professor of Economics, Augusta University, Augusta, GA, USA. He is the author and coauthor of numerous peer-reviewed articles and books, and is the cofounder and former coeditor of *The Economics of Peace and Security Journal*. His recent work has focused on the economics of the firearms industry and, with Charles Anderton, on the economics of mass atrocities and their prevention.

Christopher J. Coyne is Professor of Economics at George Mason University, Fairfax, VA, USA, and the Associate Director of the F. A. Hayek Program for Advanced Study in Philosophy, Politics, and Economics at the Mercatus Center. He is associate editor of *The Economics of Peace and Security Journal* and the author or coauthor of several books, including, most recently, *Manufacturing Militarism: U.S. Government Propaganda in the War on Terror* (Stanford University Press, 2021).

J. Paul Dunne is Emeritus Professor of Economics at the University of Cape Town, South Africa, and Emeritus Professor of Economics at the University of the West of England, Bristol, UK. He is coeditor of *The Economics of Peace and Security Journal* and a widely published global authority on economics and security.

Shikha Basnet Silwal is Associate Professor of Economics at Washington and Lee University, Lexington, VA, USA. She is associate editor of *The Economics of Peace and Security Journal* and coordinator of the annual Himalayan Policy Research Conference, typically held as a part of the Annual Conference on South Asia at the University of Wisconsin, Madison, WI, USA.

Cambridge Elements ☰

Defence Economics

Keith Hartley

University of York

Keith Hartley was Professor of Economics and Director of the Centre for Defence
Economics at the University of York, where he is now Emeritus Professor of Economics.
He is the author of over 500 publications comprising journal articles, books
and reports. His most recent books include *The Economics of Arms* (Agenda Publishing,
2017) and with Jean Belin (Eds) *The Economics of the Global Defence Industry* (Taylor and
Francis, 2020). Hartley was founding Editor of the journal *Defence and Peace Economics*;
a NATO Research Fellow; a QinetiQ Visiting Fellow; consultant to the UN, EC, EDA, UK MoD,
HM Treasury, Trade and Industry, Business, Innovation and Skills and International
Development and previously Special Adviser to the House of Commons Defence
Committee.

About the Series

Defence Economics is a relatively new field within the discipline of economics.
It studies all aspects of the economics of war and peace. It embraces a wide range of
topics in both macroeconomics and microeconomics. Cambridge Elements in Defence
Economics aims to publish original and authoritative papers in the field. These will
include expert surveys of the foundations of the discipline, its historical development
and contributions developing new and novel topics. They will be valuable contributions
to both research and teaching in universities and colleges, and will also appeal to other
specialist groups comprising politicians, military and industrial personnel as well as
informed general readers.

Cambridge Elements ≡

Defence Economics

Printed in the United States
by Baker & Taylor Publisher Services